Study Guide to Accompany

MATHEWS AND FOX'S

The Physiological Basis of Physical Education and Athletics

DONALD H. PATERSON, Ph.D.
The University of Western Ontario
London, Ontario, Canada

DAVID A. CUNNINGHAM, Ph.D.
The University of Western Ontario
London, Ontario, Canada

1977

W. B. SAUNDERS COMPANY
Philadelphia • London • Toronto

W.B.Saunders Company: West Washington Square
Philadelphia, PA 19105

1 St. Anne's Road
Eastbourne, East Sussex BN21 3UN, England

833 Oxford Street
Toronto, Ontatio M8Z 5T9, Canada

Study Guide for
THE PHYSIOLOGICAL BASIS OF PHYSICAL EDUCATION AND ATHLETICS 0-7216-7114-4

Press of W.B.Saunders Company.

Last digit is the print number: 9 8 7 6 5 4 3 2 1

PREFACE

The Study guide to the text The Physiological Basis of Physical Education and Athletics is designed to aid undergraduate students in organizing, assimilating and learning of the text material.

The Study guide is composed of a 'learning' module to accompany each chapter of the text. Each module lists the objectives of the chapter or module, provides exercises to aid students in assimilating the text material and a self-test for the students to evaluate their comprehension. Some Study guide modules contain supplementary material to aid understanding of a text chapter. The Study guide also contains a self-test at the end of each of the seven Sections included in the text.

Objectives

The objectives, listed at the beginning of each chapter or module, provide an outline of the content you will be expected to understand at the end of the module. Read each objective carefully before you begin the assignments. Concentrate on the portions of the reading that will help you most in completing the objectives. In order to focus your reading, the objectives indicate the most important parts of each chapter. It should be noted, however, that although certain sections are singled out as important all parts of a chapter or module might be necessary for a complete understanding of the problems.

Most of the objectives are the cognitive type; few require the student to manipulate the material extensively or use the information to predict answers to new problems. Note also, that each chapter of the text is followed by a series of questions, the formulation of answers to these questions will aid in the comprehension of the materials and the realization of the stated objectives.

Reading Assignment

All reading assignments are from the text "The Physiological Basis of Physical Education and Athletics" by Mathews and Fox.

Supplementary Materials

Occasionally a module contains material that can best be mastered with supplementary materials which are given in the Study guide.

Exercises

Each module contains exercises designed to aid you in digesting the material read and applying the knowledge gained.

Self-Test

Each module or chapter section contains a self-test. Take the test and if you have mastered the material in this self-testing section move on to the next section. The self-tests include objective questions of the following types:

Type 1

Directions: Each of the questions or incomplete statements below is followed by five suggested answers or completions. Select the one that is best in each case.

Example

The research of K. H. Cooper, as described in his book Aerobics, indicates that regular strenuous exercise may be medically beneficial not only as a therapeutic tool, but also in terms of:

a. preventive medicine
b. increasing the efficiency of the heart
c. improving the distribution of the blood in response to exercise
d. improving the peripheral utilization of oxygen
e. all of the above

Answer e

Type 2

Directions: This section of the test consists of situations, each follow by a series of questions. Study each situation, and select the one best answer to each question.

Example

An individual exercises for five minutes on a bicycle ergometer at a work load of 300 kgm/min.

1. His approximate oxygen uptake (litres/min) would be

   a. 0.2
   b. 0.9
   c. 0.5
   d. 1.5
   e. 2.0

   Answer b

Type 3

Directions: The following paired statements describe two entities that are to be compared in a quantitative sense.

Answer: A if (a) is greater than (b)
B if (b) is greater than (a)
C if the two are equal or very nearly equal

1. a. partial pressure of oxygen in the alveoli
b. partial pressure of oxygen in the inspired air

Answer - B

Type 4

Directions: For each of the incomplete statements below, ONE OR MORE of the completions given is correct.

Answer: A if only 1, 2 and 3 are correct
B if only 1 and 3 are correct
C if only 2 and 4 are correct
D if only 4 is correct
E if all are correct

Transport of carbon dioxide by the blood

1. involves the physical absorption of CO_2 in plasma and red blood cells

2. occurs mostly in the form of bicarbonate located in the plasma

3. involves binding to hemoglobin to form carbaminohemoglobin

4. requires carbonic anhydrase in the red blood cell for maximum efficiency.

Answer - E

Following each section is an additional self-test composed of typical questions encompassing the unit. Take the test after completing the section and (if you don't mark the page) combine the section tests to give a 'final' test following completion of the text and Study guide. The section self-tests include the same types of objective questions as listed above.

CONTENTS

Section 4

PHYSICAL TRAINING

Section 5

ENVIRONMENTAL ASPECTS

Section 6

NUTRITION AND BODY COMPOSITION

Section 7

SPECIAL CONSIDERATIONS

Module 1

INTRODUCTION

Read pages 1 - 6 for general understanding of the material to be covered in the text.

SECTION 1

BIOENERGETICS

Module 2

ENERGY SOURCES

Module 3

RECOVERY FROM EXERCISE

Module 4

ENERGY, WORK, AND POWER

Module 2

ENERGY SOURCES

Objectives

Upon completion of this module the student will be able to:

1. Define energy. List the six forms of energy. State the energy transformation most involved in human movement.
2. Outline the biological energy cycle, the process of photosynthesis and cellular respiration.
3. Name the immediate source of energy for muscular contraction and write the equation of its breakdown or energy release.
4. List the three ways by which ATP may be supplied to the muscle cell.
5. Show how phosphocreatine is used to resynthesize ATP and record the total quantity of useful energy the phosphogens may release.
6. Make a table to compare the metabolic pathways of ATP formation with regard to oxygen required, food fuel, end-products and energy or ATP released.
7. Define anaerobic and aerobic and list the energy system(s) for each.
8. Show how lactic acid is formed, including the quantity of energy liberated for every glucose molecule metabolized. Identify the factor which limits the quantity of energy production from anaerobic glycolysis.
9. Name the end-products of the oxygen system conversion of foodstuffs, and the two series of reactions involved in the aerobic pathway. Write the overall equation of oxidation of glucose. State the quantity of oxygen required to produce 1 ATP, and the quantity of energy liberated for every glucose molecule oxidized.
10. Describe the Krebs cycle and electron transport system in the oxidation of glucose.
11. Name the energy system that supplies ATP in rest and the food fuel utilized.
12. Name the food fuel and energy system which supply ATP in exercises of (a) short duration, high intensity (b) prolonged submaximal exercise. Identify the limiting factor(s) of each exercise.
13. Define oxygen deficit.

14. Identify the time duration during which both aerobic and anaerobic systems are of nearly equal importance in energy supply.

Reading Assignment

Chapter 2, pp. 9-30.

Exercises

1. Complete the following table after referring to Tables 2.1, 2.2, 2.3, 2.4, 2.5.

	Mechanism of ATP Formation	Food or Chemical Fuel	O_2 Required (Yes/no)	ATP Produced (few/many)	Useful energy (kcal for total muscle mass)	Maximal Power Capacity (high, medium, low)	
ANAEROBIC							
1.	______	______	______	______	______	______	______
2.	______	______	______	______	______	______	______
AEROBIC							
1.	______	______	______	______	______	______	______

2. Complete the diagrams of breakdown of glycogen by the aerobic and anaerobic methods.

Aerobic:

Glycogen

↓

______

______ + ______

with O_2

↓

______ + ______ + ______

Anaerobic:

Glycogen

↓

______

______ + ______

with insufficient O_2

↓

______

Check with Figure 2.4

3. In aerobic glycolysis describe the oxidation of glucose in the Krebs cycle and electron transport system.

4. Complete the following diagram to describe the percentage contribution of aerobic and anaerobic energy sources to exercise of different time durations.

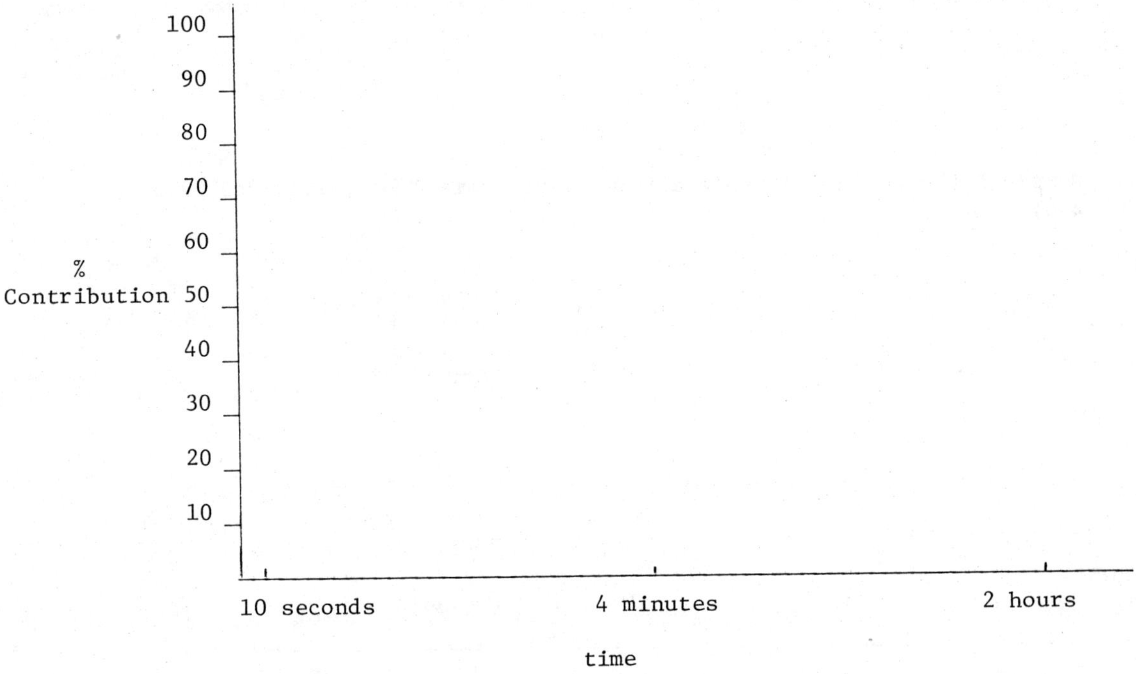

Self-Test

Part I

1. Food, the indirect source of energy, is converted through a number of chemical reactions or metabolic pathways to the immediate source of energy for muscular contraction, ______________________ or in short form ____________. This source of ______________ energy can then be transformed to ________________________ energy of movement. The chemical energy is released by breaking of the ______________________________ bond. The chemical reaction can be written as: ____.

2. The most rapidly available source of ATP for use by muscle is from the ______________ system. The chemical reactions for ATP formation can be written as: ____________________________ and ______________ ________________. PC is stored in the ________________. Energy production by this system can sustain exercise for a time period of ______________________. It is limited by the total supply of ATP and PC, the ________________.

3. In anaerobic glycolysis the food fuel is ______________________ which is partially broken down to an end product of ______________ with the liberation of ____________ ATP for each glucose molecule. This system of energy production lasts for a time period of ______ ______________________. It is limited by ______________________.

4. Aerobic breakdown of glucose follows two series of reactions known as the ________________ and ______________. The chemical reaction of glucose breakdown and the quantity of ATP liberated can be written as: ____.
From this equation calculations were shown to demonstrate that 1 mole ATP production required ______________ 1 of O_2. The limit of the aerobic pathway may be

____

____

____

Athletes have a greater oxygen consumption than non-athletes. For example for male athletes approximately ____________________ 1/min and for sedentary males _____________ 1/min.

5. At rest ATP is supplied by the ____________________ pathway with food fuel fractions being approximately ____________ fat and ____________ glucose. In the 400 m run most energy is supplied via the ____________________ pathway. Although the aerobic pathway is utilized it is slow to develop to maximal levels and even at maximal levels its ______________ (power or capacity) could not meet the energy requirements. Thus the __________________ pathway supplies ATP to cover the so called ________________________. The speed for a 400 m run cannot be maintained for 800m since the anaerobic energy supply is limited by __________________. A four minute miler derives approximately ____________% of energy from anaerobic sources and ____________% from aerobic sources. An 11 minute miler derives approximately ______________% from anerobic sources and ______________% from aerobic sources.

Part II

1. ATP may be supplied to the muscle cell by

   1. the oxygen system
   2. the lactic acid system
   3. the ATP-PC system
   4. photosynthesis with glycogen as the food fuel

   A = 1,2,3; B = 1,3; C = 2,4; D = 4; E = 1,2,3 & 4.

2. Anaerobic glycolysis

   1. provides a relatively rapid supply of ATP to sustain intense exercise for 2 to 3 minutes at which time exercise is terminated due to depletion of glycogen stores
   2. uses one mole of glucose in producing 38 ATP
   3. is the metabolic pathway whereby glucose (or glycogen) is partially metabolized to a final end product of pyruvic acid.
   4. results in a lactic acid accumulation

   A = 1,2,3; B = 1,3; C = 2,4; D = 4; E = 1,2,3 & 4.

3. The power of the oxygen system is:

   1. half that of the ATP-PC system
   2. a function of the total quantity of glucose or glycogen available as a fuel.
   3. twice that of the ATP-PC system
   4. dependent on the maximal oxygen uptake which may be 5 l/min in male athletes and only 3.2 l/min in sedentary young men.

   A = 1,2,3; B = 1,3; C = 2,4; D = 4; E = 1,2,3 & 4.

4. In rest, energy is supplied by:

   a. the ATP-PC system
   b. anaerobic glycolysis with the food fuel 2/3 fat and 1/3 glucose
   c. both the aerobic system and ATP-PC system
   d. the aerobic pathway with the food fuel 2/3 fat and 1/3 glucose
   e. the aerobic pathway with the food fuel 2/3 glycogen and 1/3 blood glucose

Answers to Self-Test on Module 2 - Energy Sources

Part I

1. adenosine triphosphate
   ATP
   chemical
   mechanical
   high energy phosphate bond
   ATP $\rightleftarrows$ ADP + Pi + energy

2. ATP - PC
   PC $\rightleftarrows$ C+Pi + energy and ADP + energy + Pi $\rightleftarrows$ ATP
   muscle cells
   only a few seconds
   phosphogens

3. glucose or glycogen
   lactic acid
   2
   2 or 3 minutes
   lactic acid accumulation in the muscle

4. Krebs cycle and electron transport system
   $C_6H_{12}O_6 + 6O_2 + 38\ ADP + 38Pi \rightleftarrows 6CO_2 + 6H_2O + 38\ ATP$
   3.5
   depletion of glycogen
   loss of water and electrolytes with high body temperature
   boredom and physical wear
   5.0
   3.2

5. aerobic
   2/3
   1/3
   anaerobic
   power
   anaerobic
   oxygen deficit
   accumulation of lactic acid
   50, 50
   30, 70

Part II

1. A = 1, 2, 3
2. D = 4
3. D = 4
4. d

Module 3

RECOVERY FROM EXERCISE

Objectives

Upon completion of this module the student will be able to:

1. Identify the metabolic energy pathway utilized during recovery.
2. Define oxygen debt and name the two components of the oxygen debt.
3. Identify the energy source which is replenished during the alactacid oxygen debt component, the time period for this replenishment and the maximal value of the alactic oxygen debt.
4. Describe how muscle glycogen is restored following exercise and how muscle glycogen stores can be built to higher than normal levels prior to competition.
5. Describe the probable mechanism of lactic acid removal during the recovery period.
6. Describe the time course of the lactacid oxygen debt component and how this recovery period can be hastened.
7. State values for the total oxygen debt and discuss the practical meaning of being able to incur a large oxygen debt or tolerate high lactic acid concentrations.

Reading Assignment

Chapter 3, pp. 31-43.

Supplementary Materials

The elevated oxygen uptake after exercise, or the oxygen debt, is related to four factors:

1. refilling the oxygen content of the body (myoglobin stores)
2. aerobic removal of anaerobic metabolites
3. elevated metabolism due to increased tissue temperature
4. oxygen demand of the still activated respiratory muscles and heart.

Exercises

1. Label the following diagram: 1 ______________________

2 ______________________

3 ______________________

4 ______________________

5 ______________________

4 + 5= ______________________

Add to the diagram the time for the point shown on the x axis in the recovery section.

6 ______________________

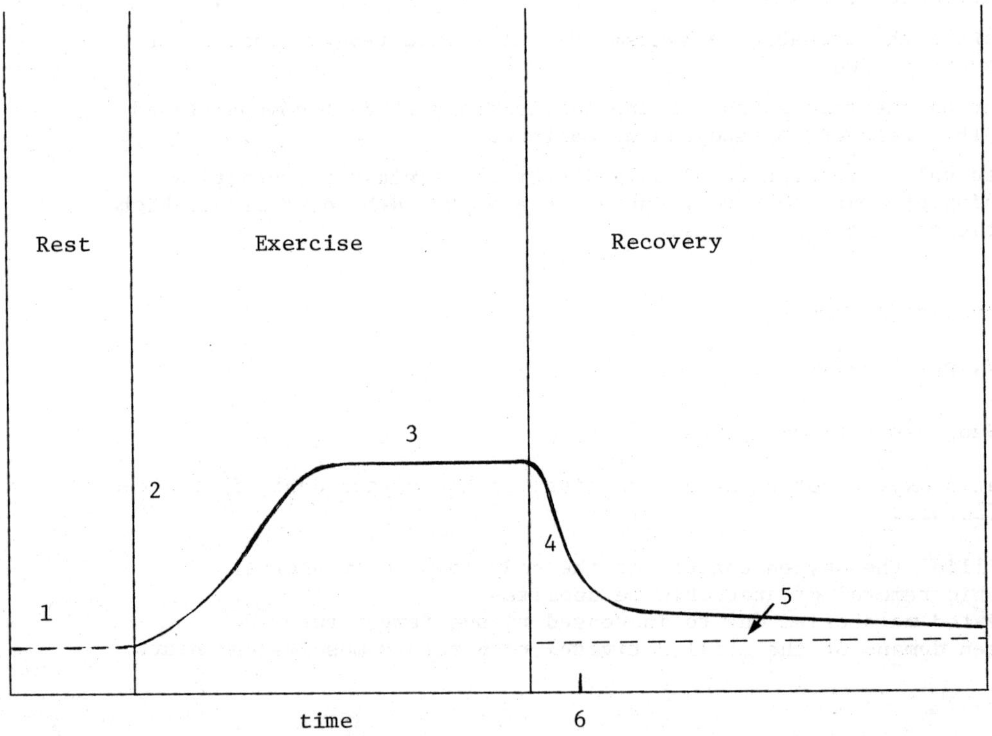

Refer to diagrams 2.10 and 3.1 as a check.

2. Describe the final week of a diet exercise regimen in preparation for a marathon run on a Saturday.

Day	Diet	Exercise
Sun. and Mon.		
Tues. or Wed.		
Thur. and Fri.		
Sat. (marathon)		

Self-Test

1. Following intense short duration activity phosphogen restoration occurs

   1. with energy supplied by the aerobic breakdown of food stuffs to CO_2 and H_2O in the Krebs cycle and electron transport system; requiring approximately 2 to 2 1/2 l of O_2

   2. within the first three minutes with half of the phosphagen restoration complete in 20 seconds

   3. during the alactacid O_2 debt component

   4. with energy supplied by the lactacid oxygen debt

   A = 1,2,3; B = 1,3; C = 2,4; D = 4; E = 1,2,3 & 4.

2. Calculate from the following example the alactacid and lactacid oxygen debt components and the total oxygen debt. Resting oxygen consumption over five minutes was 1.5 l. (or 0.3 l/min). Following a two minute run on an inclined treadmill total oxygen consumption was measured for 15 minutes. Measurements made over three minute periods were as follows:

0-3 min.	3.5 l
3-6 min.	3.0 l
6-9 min.	2.8 l
9-12 min.	2.5 l
12-15 min.	2.2 l

	Alactacid O_2 Debt	Lactacid O_2 Debt	Total O_2 Debt
A.	2.6 l/min.	6.9 l/min.	9.5 l/min.
B.	3.5 l	10.5 l	14.0 l
C.	2.0 l	9.0 l	12.5 l
D.	2.6 l	6.9 l	9.5 l
E.	3.5 l/min.	10.5 l/min.	14.0 l/min.

3. During the lactacid O_2 debt component the following occurs:

1. muscle glycogen stores depleted during exercise are resynthesized from lactic acid.

2. lactic acid build up in the muscle during exercise is carried by the circulation to the liver where it is converted to glucose.

3. lactic acid is produced in the muscles and stored to supply energy for another short burst of intense exercise.

4. lactic acid is oxidized via the oxygen system to CO_2 and H_2O with the production of ATP.

A = 1,2,3; B = 1,3; C = 2,4; D = 4; E = 1,2,3 & 4.

4. You know the time course for lactic acid removal following exercise. (a) Do you think that Olympic swimmer C. Ender's performance of events each two minutes duration and separated by less than 30 minutes was a surprising feat? (b) If you were her coach what would you have suggested immediately following the first race? Why?

Answers to Self-Test on Module 3 - Recovery from Exercise

1. A = 1,2,3
2. d Recovery 1-3 min 3.5 l - 0.9 l for 3 min rest = 2.6 l
   Recovery 3-15 min 10.5 l - 3.6 l for 12 min rest = 6.9 l
   Total 15 min 14.0 l - 4.5 l for 15 min rest = 9.5 l.
3. C = 2,4
4. (a) Yes: The 1/2 time for lactic acid removal is 15 minutes. Thus if following the first race lactic acid was 120 mg/100 ml of blood, following 15 minutes it would be 60 mg/100 ml and following 30 minutes 30 mg/100 ml.
   (b) See p. 39-40.

Module 4

ENERGY, WORK, AND POWER

Objectives

Upon completion of this module the student will be able to:

1. Define energy, work and power.
2. (a) Describe how energy is measured in a bomb calorimeter and why this is referred to as a direct method of measurement; (b) Describe the indirect measurement of energy and state the units of measure used; (c) Explain the differences between direct and indirect calorimetry.
3. (a) List the heat energy equivalents when 1 l of oxygen is used in breaking down carbohydrates, fats and proteins (i.e.: kcal/l of O_2); (b) List the heat energy equivalents per gram of carbohydrate, fat and protein metabolized.
4. Define the respiratory exchange ratio (R). List the R values when metabolizing pure carbohydrate, pure fat, and when energy is derived from a mixed diet.
5. Describe the factors other than the oxidation of food which affect the R value. In each case show how the R value changes.
6. Outline the method of determining the net energy cost of a given exercise. Describe how the procedure is simplified in measuring the energy cost of steady state sub-maximal exercise.
7. Identify the required measurements to determine oxygen consumption.
8. Define efficiency and the usual human efficiency in activities involving large muscle groups.
9. Show how work output is calculated on a bicycle ergometer, from the flywheel radius, number of pedal revolutions and given resistance on the flywheel.
10. Describe how work output is determined for an inclined treadmill.
11. Identify two ways by which oxygen consumption or work is expressed relative to body size.
12. List average values for resting ventilation, oxygen consumption and heart rate.
13. Describe the physiological considerations which allow estimation of energy cost from heart rate telemetry.

Reading Assignment

Chapter 4, pp. 44-74.

Exercises

1. With a subject riding a bicycle ergometer in a bomb calorimeter there was a heat production of 48.3 kcal in 5 minutes. What was the average oxygen consumption <u>per minute</u> knowing that metabolism was of a mixed diet?

2. (a) For a bicycle ergometer, calculate the work load in foot-pounds/min for a bike with flywheel radius of 38 inches loaded with a resistance (F) of 4.4 pounds and with the subject riding at 50 flywheel rpm. Using table 4.1 or 4.2 convert this to kg.m/min.

   (b) For a bicycle ergometer, calculate the work load in kg.m/min for a bike with flywheel circumference of 6m loaded with a resistance of 2kg and with the subject riding at 50 rpm.

3. The oxygen cost of the above exercise (2a or 2b) was 1.5 l/min. If the subject rode for 5 minutes and the R was 0.82 what was the energy input in kcal.

4. From questions 2 and 3 with reference to table 4-2, calculate the efficiency of exercise, from the total work performed and total energy required.

5. Express the following oxygen consumptions per kilogram body weight and per meter squared of body surface area, for a male subject of 70 kg of height 180 cm.

   300ml/min = ml/kg. min = ml/m^2. min

   2000ml/min = ml/kg. min = ml/m^2. min

   4000ml/min = ml/kg. min = ml/m^2. min

6. A subject was tested on a treadmill. At a heart rate of 140 b/min his oxygen consumption was 1.70 l/min. At a heart rate of 170 b/min his oxygen consumption was 2.30 l/min. What was his average oxygen consumption in a soccer game where his average heart rate measured by telemetry was 160 b/min?

Self-Test

1. A man sets out to lose weight by walking one mile every day. He walks at a normal pace of 1 mile in 15 min. His average oxygen consumption at this task is 1.2 l/min. Approximately, how many days or miles will he have to go to lose 5 pounds assuming he does not change his diet? (Assume an R of 0.82). (Remember one pound of fat is equivalent to approximately 4000 kcal).

   a. 46
   b. 260
   c. 230
   d. 100
   e. 220

2. An athletic subject rides a bicycle ergometer at 60 rpm with a weight or resistance on the flywheel of 6 kg. The flywheel circumference is 6m. What is the workload?

a. 2160 kg.m/min.
b. 360 m
c. 2160 kg.
d. 360 kg.m/min.
e. 2160 foot pounds

3. The oxygen cost of the above exercise was 4.8 l/min. If the subject continued the ride for 5 minutes and the CO_2 production was 4.8 l/min calculate the energy input in kcal.

a. 115.92 kcal
b. 24.24 kcal
c. 121.20 kcal
d. 22.78 kcal.
e. None of the above.

4. From 2 and 3, what was the approximate efficiency of the exercise performed?

a. 4%
b. 21%
c. 22%
d. 23%
e. 24%

5. Resting oxygen consumption of a swimmer was found to be 0.30 l/min. During a 400m swim heart rate averaged 180 b/min which from a previous treadmill study was equal to an oxygen uptake of 2.5 l/min. The total swim took 5 minutes. Oxygen uptake was also measured for 30 min after the swim and totalled 12 l. What was the net cost of the exercise in l of O_2?

a. 24.5 l.
b. 12.5 l.
c. 14.5 l.
d. 14.0 l.
e. cannot be determined.

6. The net oxygen consumption during a race was 20 l. The (net) oxygen debt was 5 l. Calculate the aerobic and anaerobic energy contributions.

a. Almost 100% anaerobic
b. Almost 100% aerobic
c. 20% aerobic and 80% anaerobic
d. 20% anaerobic and 80% aerobic
e. 25% anaerobic and 75% aerobic

Answers to Self-Test on Module 4 - Energy, Work and Power

1. c
2. a
3. c
4. b
5. d
6. d

SECTION 1

BIOENERGETICS

Self-Test

1. PC

   1. is stored in the muscle cells and contains two high energy phosphate bonds.

   2. can be used to provide energy for resynthesis of ATP from ADP and Pi.

   3. is the immediate source of energy for metabolic processes and the most rapidly available metabolic pathway.

   4. is resynthesized during recovery from exercise, using energy derived from ATP formed by aerobic breakdown of foodstuffs.

   A = 1,2,3; B = 1,3; C = 2,4; D = 4; E = 1,2,3 & 4.

2. The lactic acid system

   1. Contributes more than 95% of the energy requirement for a one minute all out run

   2. uses one mole of glucose in producing 2 ATP.

   3. uses primarily fat as a food fuel.

   4. is restored during the lactacid debt component of recovery with a half time of lactic acid removal of approximately 15 minutes.

   A = 1,2,3; B = 1,3; C = 2,4; D = 4; E = 1,2,3 & 4.

3. For the oxygen system

   1. the final end products of glucose breakdown are CO_2 and H_2O

   2. glucose after conversion to pyruvic acid is oxidized in the Krebs cycle and electron transport system

   3. better utilization is made of the oxygen available by the consumption of carbohydrates as opposed to fats

   4. one mole of glucose produces 38 ATP.

   A = 1,2,3; B = 1,3; C = 2,4; D = 4; E = 1,2,3 & 4.

4. The oxygen debt

   1. is the oxygen consumed during recovery above that which would be consumed in normal rest

   2. appears to have two components; the fast alactacid debt component and the slower lactacid debt component

   3. utilizes the aerobic pathway to supply energy to restore the energy stores depleted in exercise, and remove lactic acid accumulated during exercise

   4. will last less than 3 minutes if during the previous exercise none of the energy was derived from the lactic acid system.

   A = 1,2,3; B = 1,3; C = 2,4; D = 4; E = 1,2,3 & 4.

5. Which of the following statements is/are valid?

   1. at the breaking of the tape, a 4 min. miler has depleted his phosphagen resources, attained a maximum oxygen consumption, and incurred a degree of lactic acid build-up at the extremes of tolerance

   2. glycogen once converted to pyruvic acid is oxidized in the Krebs cycle and electron transport system provided there is sufficient oxygen supply

   3. the oxygen debt is equivalent to the oxygen deficit contracted during exercise and consists of a fast alactacid and slower lactacid debt component

   4. anaerobic glycolysis provides a relatively rapid supply of ATP to sustain intense exercise for 2 to 3 minutes when exercise is terminated due to depletion of glycogen stores.

   A = 1,2,3; B = 1,3; C = 2,4; D = 4; E = 1,2,3 & 4.

6. In steady state submaximal exercise oxygen consumption was measured as 2.5 l/min. CO_2 output was also measured as 2.5 l/min. What was the energy input to do such work for half an hour?

   a. 375 to 380 kcal
   b. 360 to 365 kcal
   c. 360 to 365 kcal/min
   d. 125 to 130 kcal
   e. 15 kcal/min.

7. Resting oxygen consumption of a subject was 0.3 l/min. During intense activity lasting two minutes the total oxygen consumption averaged 2.0 l/min. In the 15 minute recovery period the total oxygen debt was 16.5 l. Calculate the net oxygen cost of the exercise.

a. 16.0 l
b. 12.0 l
c. 15.4 l
d. 13.9 l
e. 18.5 l

8. From the above example calculate the percentage aerobic and anaerobic contributions.

a. almost 100% anaerobic
b. almost 100% aerobic
c. 25% aerobic and 75% anaerobic
d. 22% aerobic and 78% anaerobic
e. none of the above.

9. Calculate the percent efficiency of a 10 minute swim where the external work was calculated as 12 kcal/min and energy input totalled 3000 kcal.

a. 4
b. 21
c. 25
d. 40
e. none of the above.

10. In a six mile race a 50 kg woman had a time of 30 minutes. Her average oxygen consumption was 60 ml/kg.min. What was her caloric expenditure during the race assuming a mixed diet? (approximately).

a. 400 kcal
b. 14-15 kcal/min
c. 860 kcal
d. 11-12 kcal/min
e. 16 to 17 kcal/min

Answers to Self-Test on SECTION 1 - BIOENERGETICS

1. C = 2,4
2. C = 2,4
3. E = 1,2,3 & 4
4. E = 1,2,3 & 4
5. A = 1,2,3
6. a
7. c
8. d
9. a
10. b

SECTION 2

NEUROMUSCULAR CONCEPTS

Module 5

NERVOUS CONTROL OF MUSCULAR MOVEMENT

Module 6

SKELETAL MUSCLE: STRUCTURE AND FUNCTION

Module 7

MUSCULAR STRENGTH, ENDURANCE, AND FLEXIBILITY

Module 5

NERVOUS CONTROL OF MUSCULAR MOVEMENT

Objectives

Upon completion of this module the student will be able to:

1. Describe the function of sensory nerves, the central nervous system and motor nerves. Name the three basic functions of the nervous system.
2. Identify the sensory receptors for smell, sound and balance.
3. Give the collective name for the nerve fibres which (a) transmit a sensory stimulus to the spinal cord and (b) transmit impulses from the central nervous system (CNS) to the appropriate muscles; (c) Describe the simple reflex arc.
4. Diagram and label the parts of a nerve cell.
5. Outline the process of transmission from one nerve to another, including a definition of the EPSP. Define spacial summation and temporal summation.
6. Describe how inhibition may occur at the neuronal synapse, and outline the function (or value) of this inhibitory mechanism.
7. Describe signal transmission at the neuromuscular junction.
8. Identify the components of a single motor unit.
9. Describe the function of proprioceptors and identify the location of proprioceptors.
10. Draw and label a muscle spindle.
11. Describe the activation of motor neurons that cause the muscle to contract by (a) tonic stretch (b) phasic stretch (c) the gamma loop. Describe the overall affect of these controls on muscular contraction.
12. Describe the stretch reflex and give examples of neuromuscular stretch reflexes.
13. (a) Outline the role of internuncial neurons and ascending and descending nerve fibres in the CNS. (b) Describe the function of the primary motor cortex and premotor area. (c) Describe the function of the motor cortex and cerebellum in the control of motor functions.
14. State what an engram is and differentiate between sensory and motor engrams.
15. Outline the Henry memory drum theory of motor learning.

Reading Assignment

Chapter 5, pp. 77-100

Exercises

1. In the simple reflex arc impulses from ____________ receptors are transmitted to the __________ by ______________ nerves which synapse with _____________ nerve fibres to transmit the impulse to appropriate muscles.

2. At the synaptic cleft a chemical transmitter called ____________________ is discharged resulting in an increased electrical potential in the __________________ neuron. If the __________________________ is greater than 11 millivolts or the _____________, the signal is transmitted. When stimuli are received from various pre-synaptic terminals it is called ___________________________. If the same pre-synaptic terminal emits successive discharges they may cause neuronal discharge by ____________________________.

3. Nerve to muscle transmission occurs at the ________________________. Again ________ is secreted at the synaptic cleft. Following stimulation the acetylcholine is absorbed by ____________________ to prevent continued exitation. An individual nerve fibre plus all the muscle fibres it innervates is called a __________________.

4. Proprioceptors located in (1) ____________, (2) ______________ (3) ______________ and (4) ____________ provide information of __________________________________ often called ____________________________________. Proprioceptors in the muscle are called the _____________________. These modified muscle cells called _______________ fibres are not contractile in the centre portion. Their motor innervation is from ___________________________ as opposed to _______________________ innervating the extrafusal fibres. The muscle spindle is sensitive to both ___________ and _____________________________ of the muscle fibres. Stretch of the muscle activates ______________ nerves which send the impulse to the central nervous system.

   The muscle spindle may also be stimulated directly by ______________________ from impulses sent directly from the motor cortex. In response to information of muscle stretch impulses from the muscle spindle synapse with motor nerve cells in the spinal cord and activation of the motor endplates produces ________________ to oppose the stretch.

5. There is a section in the brain called the ________________ which transmits impulses down the ______________ tract to the muscles. Impulses are also sent to the _________________. As the movement is executed the cerebellum receives feedback and compares the two sets of information to correct the movement pattern.

6. It appears that memorized motor patterns called ____________ may be stored in the ____________ area of the brain. Thus, upon appropriate stimulus the pattern can be recalled. It also appears that there may be ________________ to allow extremely rapid movements. Thus motor acts may be stored on a so called memory drum. It thus appears that motor ability is ____________ to a task.

Self-Test

1. A post-synaptic neuron discharges when:

   a. sufficient calcium is released into the synaptic cleft to create an electrical potential above the threshold EPSP

   b. both the CNS and reflex arc provide the same input

   c. sufficient ACh is released into the synaptic cleft to create an electrical potential above the threshold EPSP

   d. afferent fibres from the muscle spindle detect stretch of the extrafusal muscle fibres

   e. more than two pre-synaptic nerves release ACh into the synaptic cleft.

2. Proprioceptors are located in:

   1. muscles
   2. tendons
   3. ligaments
   4. joints

   A = 1,2,3; B = 1,3; C = 2,4; D = 4; E = 1,2,3 & 4.

3. When a muscle is stretched

   1. the intrafusal fibres are also stretched and activated sensory nerves send impulses to the CNS which in turn activates the alpha motor neuron to cause the muscle to contract

   2. the gamma motor neurons detect the change in length and this sensory input causes the muscle to contract

   3. a simple stretch reflex may occur where afferent fibres from the muscle spindle transmit impulses to the spinal cord and motor fibres activate the stretched muscle fibres causing them to contract

4. the primary motor cortex sends impulses along the pyramidal tract and to the cerebellum and the appropriate muscles are excited

A = 1,2,3; B = 1,3; C = 2,4; D = 4; E = 1,2,3 & 4.

4. There is a theory regarding the manner by which skills are memorized. Which of the following are correct?

1. according to the theory movement patterns are stored in what might be called a memory drum

2. the theory is referred to as Henry's Memory Drum Theory

3. support for the theory comes from, for example, the finding that the ability of a person to make fast arm movements varies with the exact movement requested

4. according to the theory motor ability is specific to the task

A = 1,2,3; B = 1,3; C = 2,4; D = 4; E = 1,2,3 & 4.

Answers to Self-Test on Module 5 - Nervous Control of Muscular Movement.

1. c
2. E = 1,2,3 & 4
3. B = 1,3
4. E = 1,2,3 & 4

Module 6

SKELETAL MUSCLE: STRUCTURE AND FUNCTION

Objectives

Upon completion of this module the student will be able to:

1. Identify the structural units and associated connective tissues of skeletal muscle - sarcoplasm, sarcolemma, endomysium, fasciculus, perimysium, epimysium.
2. Describe the origin and attachment of tendons and the muscle blood supply.
3. Describe the nerve supply of muscles and the structure and function of a motor unit.
4. Define the all or none law and name the structural unit to which the all or none law applies.
5. Describe the function of Golgi tendon organs.
6. Name the two different types of human muscle fibres. Make a chart to compare the two types under the following headings: anaerobic capability, aerobic capability, capillary density, glycogen and PC content, speed of contraction, fatigue factor, fibres preferentially used for high intensity short duration work and fibres preferentially used for endurance exercise.
7. State what determines a muscle fibre type and whether the distribution of red and white muscle fibres is affected by physical training.
8. Draw and label a sarcomere (myofibril) showing the I band, A band, Z line and H zone. Name the major protein of the thin filament of the I band and the protein which makes up the thick A band.
9. Outline the sliding filament theory of muscular contraction. Include an understanding of the role of cross-bridges, calcium, actomyosin, ATPase, ATP.

Reading Assignment

Chapter 6, pp. 101-121.

Exercises

1. Skeletal muscle is composed of thousands of __________ fibres. Each fibre is encased by ______________ tissue called the ______________. A bundle of muscle cell fibres called a ______________ is bound by connective tissue referred to as the ________________. The entire muscle is encased by a connective tissue component named the ________________. The intramuscular network of connective tissue comes together to form ____________ which attach to the ___________.

2. Muscle is supplied by both ____________ and ______________ nerve fibres. A single motor nerve may innervate from ______ to ________ muscle fibres. The single motor nerve and the muscle fibres it innervates are called the ________________. A motor unit which consists of very few muscle fibres can perform _______ ________________ movements.

3. Compare the function of muscle spindles and the Golgi tendon organs.

4. Complete the following table.

Muscle Fibre Type	Type I	Type II
Other Names	______________	______________
Aerobic capability	______________	______________
Anaerobic capability	______________	______________
Capillary density	______________	______________
Glycogen & PC content	______________	______________
Speed of contraction	______________	______________
Fatigue factor	______________	______________
Fibres for high intensity, short duration work	______________	______________
Fibres for endurance work	______________	______________

5. Draw and label a myofibril to show the I band, H zone, Z line, A band.

6. According to the sliding filament theory of muscular contraction, ________ is pulled over __________ producing shortening of the muscle. The process derives its energy from the breakdown of _____. Activation of the actin filaments requires _____________ released from the _________________.

Self-Test

1. The strength of a muscular contraction depends on

   1. the strength of the nerve impulse to a given motor unit
   2. the number of motor units stimulated
   3. the quantity of calcium released from the sarcoplasmic reticulum
   4. the number of muscle fibres per motor unit

   A = 1,2,3; B = 1,3; C = 2,4; D = 4; E = 1,2,3 & 4.

2. An endurance athlete

   1. is probably born with a greater percentage of slow-twitch fibres
   2. because of training improves the size and capacity of red muscle fibres
   3. preferentially recruits red slow-twitch fibres in the performance of a long distance run
   4. appears to be born with a higher percentage of white muscle fibres.

   A = 1,2,3; B = 1,3; C = 2,4; D = 4; E = 1,2,3 & 4.

3. Which of the following is/are correct?

   1. red, Type I fibres are preferentially recruited for sprinting performance
   2. red or tonic muscle fibres because of their greater PC content are used in postural work
   3. white, fast twitch fibres are found in greater percentage in endurance athletes than in non-endurance subjects
   4. red or slow twitch muscle fibres have a relatively high aerobic capability and fatigue slowly

   A = 1,2,3; B = 1,3; C = 2,4; D = 4: E = 1,2,3 & 4.

4. Which labelling is appropriate for the microscopic sarcomere structure:

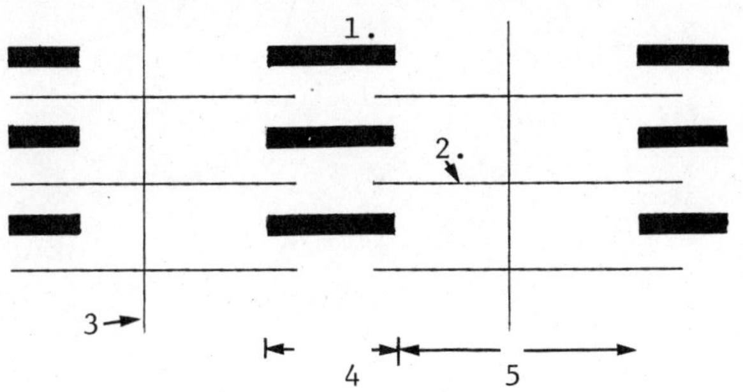

a. ^{1}myosin, ^{2}actin, ^{3}Z line, ^{4}A band, ^{5}I band
b. ^{1}actin, ^{2}myosin, ^{3}Z line, ^{4}H zone, ^{5}I band
c. ^{1}myosin, actin, ^{2}T-tubule, ^{3}A band, ^{4}I band
d. ^{1}myosin, ^{2}actin, ^{3}T-tubule, ^{4}H zone, ^{5}A band
e. ^{1}actin, ^{2}myosin, ^{3}T-tubule, ^{4}I band, ^{5}A band

5. Order the following events to describe muscular contraction according to the sliding filament theory

1. Ca^{++} is released from the sarcoplasmic reticulum and activates the actin filament and in an unknown manner the ATP cross-bridges are "charged"
2. actin and myosin are coupled activating ATPase
3. impulses from the nerve generate an action potential in the muscle fibre which is spread through the T-tubules
4. cross-bridges swivel and actin slides over myosin
5. ATP $\longrightarrow$ ADP + Pi + energy

a = 5,3,2,1,4; b = 4,3,5,2,1; c = 3,1,2,5,4; d = 3,1,2,4,5;
e = 3,5,1,2,4.

Answers to Self-Test on Module 6 - Skeletal Muscle Structure and Function

1. C = 2,4
2. A = 1,2,3
3. D = 4
4. a
5. c

Module 7

MUSCULAR STRENGTH, ENDURANCE, AND FLEXIBILITY

Objectives

Upon completion of this module the student will be able to:

1. Define lever and moment.
2. Identify the position at which an isolated muscle can exert greatest force or tension. Describe how the moment arm of force is important in determining the joint angles where muscular contraction creates the greatest moment of force, or torque.
3. Solve problems related to the principle of moments.
4. Describe the difference between strength training programs using barbells and those using Nautilus equipment, the Mini-Gym or Cybex.
5. Define the following types of muscular contractions: (a) isotonic (b) isometric (c) isokinetic. Differentiate between a concentric and eccentric contraction.
6. Identify the structural changes brought about within a muscle as a consequence of a weight training program.
7. Explain the overload principle.
8. Give different examples of the specificity of weight training.
9. Describe (a) a typical isotonic weight training program; (b) a typical isometric muscular exercise program and (c) an isokinetic muscular exercise program.
10. Describe how strength and endurance gains from weight training can be retained.
11. Identify structural limitations to flexibility.
12. Describe how flexibility can be developed and compare passive to ballistic stretching.
13. Identify whether flexibility is joint-specific or general.

Reading Assignment

Chapter 7, pp. 122-162.

Exercises

1. Answer questions 2, 3 and 4 on p. 159.

2. Describe an isokinetic exercise program to improve muscular strength.

3. Outline the principles of progressive resistance exercise (PRE) and recommendations of DeLorme for strength training.

4. List the considerations, with regard to specificity, in planning a strength training program.

5. Which type of stretching in the development of flexibility seems preferred and why?

Self-Test

1. The disadvantage of barbell weight-lifting programs is that

   a. the muscle is not continuously overloaded throughout the full range of movement.

   b. it may result in muscle fibre splitting.

   c. the hypertrophy results in a slower speed of contraction.

   d. muscular hypertrophy limits flexibility.

   e. gains in muscular strength are very quickly lost unless weight-lifting is continued throughout life.

2. Increased strength is accompanied by

   1. increase in diameter of individual muscle fibres

   2. increased amounts and strength of connective, tendinous and ligamentous tissues

   3. increased capillary density per fibre

   4. increased protein in the myosin filament

   A = 1,2,3; B = 1,3; C = 2,4; D = 4; E = 1,2,3 & 4.

3. Which of the following is/are correct?

1. the muscle shortens with varying tension while lifting a constant load = isometric contraction

2. muscle length is unchanged while tension is developed = isotonic contraction.

3. the muscle lengthens while developing tension = concentric contraction.

4. the tension developed by the muscle while shortening is maximal over the full range of motion = isokinetic contraction.

A = 1,2,3; B = 1,3; C = 2,4; D = 4; E = 1,2,3 & 4.

Answers to Self-Test on Module 7 - Muscular Strength, Endurance and Flexibility

1. a
2. E = 1,2,3 & 4
3. D = 4

Self-Test

1. In the simple reflex arc

   1. sensory input is transmitted to the CNS via the afferent nerve

   2. the sensory nerve synapses with the motor nerve in the spinal cord

   3. the afferent message is transmitted to the efferent nerve only if a threshold EPSP is reached

   4. ACh acts as the chemical transmitter at the myoneural junction.

   A = 1,2,3; B = 1,3; C = 2,4; D = 4; E = 1,2,3 & 4.

2. A motor unit:

   1. consists of all the muscle fibres innervated by a single neuron

   2. obeys the all or none law of contraction

   3. makes possible graded muscular contractions; by the number of motor units employed

   4. may consist of hundreds of muscle fibres such as in the eye muscles or only a few muscle fibres such as in the calf muscle (gastrocnemius).

   A = 1,2,3; B = 1,3; C = 2,4; D = 4; E = 1,2,3 & 4.

3. The muscle spindle

   1. is a proprioceptor

   2. responds to muscle length and phasic stretch via reflex sensory input regarding stretch of the intrafusal muscle fibres

   3. may be stimulated by the gamma loop system

   4. consists of a single nerve fibre and each of the muscle fibres it innervates

   A = 1,2,3; B = 1,3; C = 2,4; D = 4; E = 1,2,3 & 4.

4. There is a theory regarding the manner by which skills are memorized. Which of the following is/are correct?

   1. according to the theory motor ability is specific to the task

   2. according to the theory movement patterns are stored on what might be called a memory drum

   3. support for the theory comes from studies which demonstrate that a person's ability for fast arm movement varies with the exact movement requested

   4. the cerebellum stores engrams which are transmitted down the pyramidal tract to coordinate appropriate muscle responses.

   A = 1,2,3; B = 1,3; C = 2,4; D = 4; E = 1,2,3 & 4.

5. Which of the following is/are correct?

   1. the epimysium, perimysium and endomysium form tendons to connect muscle to bone

   2. graded strength of muscle contraction depends on the number of motor units stimulated.

   3. Golgi tendon proprioceptors respond to tendon stretch and may inhibit forceful muscular contraction

   4. a single muscle fibre consists of a number of myofibrils.

   A = 1,2,3; B = 1,3; C = 2,4; D = 4; E = 1,2,3 & 4.

6. Which of the following is/are correct?

   1. red or slow twitch muscle fibres have a relatively high aerobic capability and because of their high PC content are used in postural work

   2. white, fast twitch fibres are found in greater proportion in endurance athletes compared with non-endurance subjects

   3. the H zone of striated muscle consists of both myosin and actin and the I band consists of actin only

   4. in muscular contraction the actin and myosin filaments do not change length but the sarcomere is shortened with the Z lines pulled closer together.

   A = 1,2,3; B = 1,3; C = 2,4; D = 4; E = 1,2,3 &4.

7. According to the sliding filament theory of muscular contraction which of the following is/are true?

   1. calcium from the vesicles activates the actin

   2. actin and myosin come together to form actomyosin

   3. ATP breakdown provides energy

   4. the myosin cross bridges and active actin filaments "make and break" hundreds of times in a one second contraction.

   A = 1,2,3; B = 1,3; C = 2,4; D = 4; E = 1,2,3 & 4.

8. Studies of muscular strength training have suggested

   1. a superiority of isokinetic programs for both strength and endurance gains

   2. that a low repitition, high load program is effective for strength improvement but not endurance improvement

   3. that one day a week provides an adequate maintenance program

   4. eccentric contractions are extremely effective in training of athletes

   A = 1,2,3; B = 1,3; C = 2,4; D = 4; E = 1,2,3 & 4.

9. The disadvantage(s) of an isokinetic strength training program include:

   1. the muscle is not continuously overloaded throughout the full range of motion

   2. with the Nautilus equipment the cam system is suited to average muscular force at given joint angles

   3. the strength gains using such equipment as the cybex are highly specific to the speed of movement

   4. the equipment (Cybex or Nautilus) is expensive

   A = 1,2,3; B = 1,3; C = 2,4; D = 4; E = 1,2,3 & 4.

10. Flexibility

1. is joint specific

2. should be included in warm-up prior to athletic competition

3. can be improved by static stretching exercises

4. is severely limited in "musclebound" individuals

A = 1,2,3; B = 1,3; C = 2,4; D = 4; E = 1,2,3 & 4.

Answers to Self-Test on SECTION 2 - NEUROMUSCULAR CONCEPTS

1. E = 1,2,3 & 4.
2. A = 1,2,3
3. A = 1,2,3
4. A = 1,2,3
5. E = 1,2,3 & 4
6. D = 4
7. E = 1,2,3 & 4
8. B = 1,3
9. C = 2,4
10. A = 1,2,3

SECTION 3

CARDIORESPIRATORY CONSIDERATIONS

Module 8

PULMONARY VENTILATION

Module 9

GASEOUS EXCHANGE AND TRANSPORT

Module 10

BLOOD FLOW AND GAS TRANSPORT

Module 11

CARDIORESPIRATORY CONTROL

Module 8

PULMONARY VENTILATION

Objectives

Upon completion of this module the student will be able to:

1. Define minute ventilation in terms of tidal volume and respiratory rate.
2. Describe minute ventilation at rest and exercise in terms of volume size and respiratory rates. Convert minute ventilation from values ATPS to BTPS and STPD.
3. Describe the change in minute ventilation with exercise and recovery and the differences between trained and untrained subjects in their response to exercise.
4. Define the terms alveolar ventilation, and anatomic dead space and be able to describe the factors which alter these volumes.
5. Calculate alveolar ventilation given the tidal volume, rate of breathing and size of the dead space.
6. Define the basic lung volumes and describe how they change with exercise.
7. Describe "second wind" and the possible causes.
8. Explain the factors which contribute to inspiration and expiration and the factors which determine the oxygen cost of ventilation.
9. Describe the effect of cigarette smoking on the cost of ventilation.
10. Describe the intrapulmonary and intrapleural pressure changes and the movement of air into and out of the lung.
11. Correct gas volumes from values given at atmospheric temperature and pressure saturated to values at standard temperature and pressure dry or body temperature atmospheric pressure saturated.

Reading Assignment.

Chapter 8, pp. 165-184 and Appendix B, pp. 519-524.

Exercises

Directions: Complete Tables 1 and 2 to calculate alveolar ventilation. Use 150 ml as the volume for the dead space volume. In Table 2 use the frequency values given in Table 1 to calculate the dead space ventilation.

Table 1

Subject	Tidal Volume (ml/breath)	x	Frequency (breath/min)	=	Total Pulmonary Ventilation (ml/min)
A	150	x	50	=	________
B	250	x	30	=	________
C	500	x	15	=	________
D	1250	x	6	=	________

In Table 2 use the values calculated in Table 1 for the total pulmonary ventilation for subjects A through D. Again, use 150 ml as the dead-space value and the frequencies of respiration provided above.

Table 2

Subject	Total Pulmonary Ventilation	-	Dead Space Ventilation (dead space vol. x frequency, ml/breath x breath/min)	=	Alveolar Ventilation
	ml/min	-	ml/min		ml/min
A	________		________	=	0
B	7500	-	(150) x (30)	=	________
C	________	-	________	=	5250
D	________	-	900	=	6600

Self-Test

1. Minute ventilation or the amount of air expired in one minute ($\dot{V}_E$) can be calculated by multiplying

a. tidal volume x volume expired per minute
b. inhalation volume x dead space volume
c. breaths per minute x tidal volume
d. breaths per minute x dead space volume
e. breaths per minute x alveolar volume

2. The following laboratory data were obtained on two subjects

	#1	#2
Respiratory Rate	10/min	20/min
Tidal Volume	600 ml.	300 ml.
Physiologic Dead Space	150 ml.	150 ml.

Compared to Subject #2, the alveolar ventilation (in ml/min) of Subject #1 is:

a. 3 x as large
b. 2 x as large
c. 1 1/2 x as large
d. the same
e. 1/3 as large

3. The Collins spirometer can be used to measure all of the following EXCEPT

a. tidal volume
b. vital capacity
c. inspiratory reserve volume
d. functional residual capacity
e. expiratory reserve volume

4. Which of the following respiratory muscles is <u>most</u> involved in quiet inspiration

a. the internal intercostals
b. the external intercostals
c. the diaphragm
d. the rectus abdominus
e. the sternocleidomastoides

5. Calculate the volume of a gas = 150 litres (ATPS) to standard temperature and pressure dry (STPD). In this case the P_B = 750 mmHg; P_{H_2O} = 20 mmHg; and T = 21°C. The answer in litres (STPD) is

a. 152.4
b. 163.8
c. 135.6
d. 133.8
e. 125.2

6. During exercise, minute ventilation ($\dot{V}_E$) changes, these changes may be described by one or more of the following

1. there is a slow increase in ventilation starting at least 5 to 10 seconds after exercise is initiated. This increase in ventilation is probably related to stimulation arising from the joints resulting from the movement generated by the working muscles

2. there is a very rapid increase within only a few seconds after the start of exercise. This change in ventilation is probably related to stimulation from the joints resulting from the movement generated by the working muscles

3. after the initial change in ventilation a fast rise follows which in submaximal exercise tends to level off. The control of this phase is thought to originate from the chemical stimuli of the oxygen in the blood which is reduced during exercise

4. after the initial change in ventilation there is a slow rise which in submaximal exercise tends to level off. This period of slow change in ventilation is thought to be stimulated by chemical factors in the blood; mainly carbon dioxide produced during the exercise.

A = 1,2,3; B = 1,3; C = 2,4; D = 4; E = 1,2,3 & 4.

7. The following paired statement describes two entities that are to be compared in a quantitative sense.

Answer A if (a) is greater than (b)
B if (b) is greater than (a)
C if the two are equal or very nearly equal

a. intrapulmonary pressure at the onset of inspiration

b. intrapulmonary pressure at the onset of expiration

Answers to Self-Test on Module 8 - Pulmonary Ventilation

1. c
2. c
3. d
4. c
5. d
6. C = 2,4
7. C

Module 9

GASEOUS EXCHANGE AND TRANSPORT

Objectives

Upon completion of this module the student will be able to:

1. Define partial pressure of a gas and passive diffusion.
2. Describe the relationship between partial pressure and concentration of a gas.
3. List the steps in the exchange of oxygen and carbon dioxide between the atmosphere and the lungs, and between the blood and tissues.
4. List the factors which can affect gaseous exchange.
5. Describe the factors affecting diffusion capacity during exercise.
6. Compare the diffusion capacity of athletes and sedentary subjects and the effect of training on diffusion capacity.
7. List two factors which determine the amount of gas which can be dissolved in a liquid.
8. Define hemoglobin, oxyhemoglobin, reduced hemoglobin, and dissolved blood gases, and describe the role of each in the transport of gas in the blood.
9. Describe the oxygen capacity of hemoglobin and be able to calculate this value given the hemoglobin concentration and per cent saturation.
10. State the effects on the oxygen dissociation curve of changes in the acidity of the blood, the temperature of the blood or carbon dioxide tension in the blood.
11. List the three forms in which carbon dioxide is carried in the body.
12. Name the function served by carbonic anhydrase and the site of action within the body.
13. Show the relationship between CO_2 transport and acid-base balance.
14. Calculate the oxygen uptake and carbon dioxide production given the volume of air exhaled per minute, the fractional concentration of oxygen in exhaled air, the fractional concentration of oxygen in the inspired air, the fractional concentration of carbon dioxide in expired air and the fractional concentration of carbon dioxide in inspired air.

Reading Assignment

Chapter 9, pp. 185-204 and Appendix C, pp. 525-530.

Exercises

1. Atmospheric pressure at sea level is 760 mmHg. If air contains 21 per cent oxygen, what is the partial pressure of oxygen (PO_2) at sea level? ______________________.

2. PO_2 is highest in the ______________________.

3. Except for the cells PO_2 is lowest in the ______________________.

4. Except for the cells PCO_2 is highest in the ______________________.

5. PCO_2 is lowest in the ______________________.

6. Oxygen in the blood can be carried in two ways

   i combined with hemoglobin
   ii dissolved in the blood

   The percentage saturation refers to which of these? __________.

7. The percentage saturation of oxygen is affected by

   i the size of the individual
   ii temperature
   iii acidity
   iv PCO_2

Self-Test

Part I

1. The pressure of a gas is proportional to its ______________________ and ______________________.

2. The movement of molecules from an area of high concentration to an area of low concentration usually occurs passively by ______________.

3. Name two forms in which oxygen is carried in the blood.

   a. ______________________

   b. ______________________

4. Name the three forms in which carbon dioxide is carried in the blood.

   a. ______________________

   b. ______________________

   c. ______________________

5. The shift in the O_2 dissociation curve seen in exercise is important for two reasons.

a. ______________________________

____

b. ______________________________

____

Part II

1. The following paired statements describe two entities that are to be compared in a quantitative sense.

Answer A if (a) is greater than (b)
B if (b) is greater than (a)
C if the two are equal or very nearly equal

a. partial pressure of oxygen in the alveoli
b. partial pressure of oxygen in inspired air

2. The exchange of gases between the alveolar air and blood is due to:

a. active secretion
b. passive diffusion
c. osmotic pressure
d. selective excretion
e. none of the above

3. For a subject living at sea level the following information is provided:

Hemoglobin = 14 gm/100 ml. blood
Blood is 95% saturated

Which of the following values best describes the oxygen content of the arterial blood of this subject? Disregard the dissolved oxygen.

a. 20.1 ml oxygen/100ml blood
b. 17.8 ml oxygen/100ml blood
c. 16.4 ml oxygen/100ml blood
d. 15.6 ml oxygen/100ml blood
e. none of the above

Answers to Self-Test on Module 9 - Gaseous Exchange and Transport

Part I

1. concentration and speed of molecules

2. diffusion

3. a. physically dissolved in the blood
   b. chemically bound to hemoglobin

4. a. physically dissolved in blood
   b. chemically bound to hemoglobin
   c. converted into bicarbonate and hydrogen ions

5. a. because more O_2 is available to the tissues at a given tissue PO_2
   b. because the loading of blood with O_2 is not greatly affected.

Part II

1. B
2. b
3. b

Module 10

BLOOD FLOW AND GAS TRANSPORT

Objectives

Upon completion of this module the student will be able to:

1. State the two major blood flow changes which occur during exercise.
2. Define cardiac output ($\dot{Q}$), heart rate (HR) and stroke volume (SV), and identify normal values for each at rest and during light to vigorous exercise.
3. Describe how the large increases in $\dot{Q}$ during exercise are brought about and describe the different responses to exercise between trained and untrained subjects.
4. Describe the relationship between cardiac output, stroke volume and heart rate.
5. Describe the changes in stroke volume and heart rate during exercise.
6. Describe the changes in cardiac output in short and prolonged exercise.
7. Describe how blood flow is redistributed during exercise.
8. Describe the basic mechanisms which aid venous return at rest and during exercise.
9. Describe the oxygen or gas transport system in terms of cardiac output and arterial-venous oxygen difference at rest and during exercise.
10. State the two major hemodynamic factors which modify the cardiac output.
11. Define blood pressure and explain how and why it changes during exercise.
12. Describe the factors which modify resistance to blood flow.
13. Describe the changes in pressure and resistance during exercise.

Reading Assignment

Chapter 10, pp. 205-224.

Supplementary Material

1. Mean Arterial Pressure

As was described in the text the mean arterial pressure is often described as the average of the systemic systolic and diastolic pressures during a complete cardiac cycle (see page 219). In fact, the mean arterial blood pressure (MABP) is not merely the value half way between systolic and diastolic pressure, because diastole usually lasts longer than systole. Actually, the MABP can be obtained only by very complex methods, but in most instances it is reasonably accurate to assume the MABP to be the diastolic pressure plus one-third of the difference between the systolic and diastolic pressure (pulse pressure).

MABP = diastolic pressure + (1/3 pulse pressure).

<u>For example</u>:

	systolic pressure	=	130 mmHg
	diastolic pressure	=	80 mmHg
	MABP	=	96.6 mmHg
or	MABP	=	80 + (1/3 x 50)
		=	80 + 16.65
		=	96.6 mmHg.

The MABP is actually the most important of the pressures since it is the average pressure driving blood into the tissues throughout the cardiac cycle

Exercises

Part I

Directions: Fill in the appropriate numbers in the blank spaces. Use any values you wish as long as they are sensible for the condition.

1.

	$\dot{Q}$ (ml/min)	=	H.R. (beats/min)	x	SV (ml/beat)
Rest	5600	=	________	x	________
Mild Exercise	________	=	________	x	120
Vigorous Exercise	________	=	180	x	________

2.

	Oxygen Uptake ($\dot{V}O_2$) (ml/min)	=	S.V. (litres/beat)	x	H.R. (beats/min)	x	a-$\bar{v}$ O_2 diff (ml/litre)
Rest	300	=	0.080	x	________	x	________
Mild Exercise	3300	=	________	x	160	x	________
Vigorous Exercise	5600	=	.180	x	________	x	________

Would you consider the subject described in #2 to be trained or untrained if you also knew that he was 26 years of age and weighed 75 kg.?

3. Substitute the appropriate values

	Cardiac Output ($\dot{Q}$) (ml/min)	=	Mean arterial bl. Press (P) (mmHg)	/	resistance (R) (mmHg/litre/min)
Rest	5.6	=	95	/	16.9
Mild Ex.	10	=	________	/	________
Vigorous Ex.	25	=	________	/	________

Self-Test

1. In order to fully meet the gas transport demands during exercise which of the following best describe the changes in blood flow?

   1. cardiac output is increased
   2. total peripheral resistance is increased
   3. blood flow is redistributed from inactive to active organs
   4. stroke volume is decreased

   A = 1,2,3; B = 1,3; C = 2,4; D = 4; E = 1,2,3 & 4.

2. Describe the changes in cardiac output, stroke volume and heart rate during prolonged submaximal work, i.e. work over 30 minutes duration

   increased/decreased/same

   cardiac output is ____________________

   stroke volume is ____________________

   heart rate is ____________________

3. During exercise blood flow is redistributed. This redistribution involves

   a. a smaller amount of blood being directed towards the brain
   b. a larger amount of blood being directed toward the gut
   c. a larger amount of blood being directed to the active muscles
   d. a reflex vasodilation of the arterioles supplying the visceral organs
   e. both b and d.

4. In a resting subject with an oxygen consumption of 240 ml/min., the systemic arterial oxygen content is 200 ml/L. and the pulmonary arterial oxygen content is 160 ml/L. The volume of oxygen transported per minute via the arterial systemic blood is:

   a. 240 ml.
   b. 480 ml.
   c. 960 ml.
   d. 1200 ml.
   e. 2400 ml.

5. The following paired statement describes two entities that are to be compared in a quantitative sense.

   Answer A if (a) is greater than (b)
   B if (b) is greater than (a)
   C if the two are equal or very nearly equal

   a. the increase in maximal cardiac output over resting values
   b. the increase in maximal stroke volume over resting values

Answers to Self-Test of Module 10 - Blood Flow and Gas Transport

1. B = 1,3
2. same
   decreased
   increased
3. c
4. d
5. A

Module 11

CARDIORESPIRATORY CONTROL

Objectives

Upon completion of this module the student will be able to:

1. Locate the centres for respiratory and circulatory control and describe their main function.
2. State the two main types of stimuli which affect the control centres of respiration and circulation.
3. Describe the differences between neural and humoral stimuli and give examples of each.
4. Describe the action of humoral and neural stimuli on the cardiorespiratory centres and demonstrate their ability by filling in a table (receptors and location) such as Table 11-1 p. 229 of the text by Mathews and Fox.
5. Describe the effects of various stimuli on ventilation and blood flow as illustrated in Table 11-2 of Mathews and Fox.
6. Describe the different effects of sympathetic and parasympathetic nerves on cardiac function and be able to state the chemical mediators of both nerve groups.
7. Describe a negative feedback mechanism and give an example from the control of the cardiorespiratory system.
8. Describe how ventilation and blood flow are regulated during rest and exercise.

Reading Assignment

Chapter 11, pp. 225-236.

Exercises

1. Fill in the following table similar to one on page 229 (Table 11-1). Indicate whether the action is central or reflex with (x) and then name the receptor and its location.

Action of Humoral and Neural Stimuli on The Cardiorespiratory Centres

Stimuli	Action on Cardiorespiratory Centres			
	Direct (Central)	Indirect (Reflex)	Name	Location
A. Humoral				
1. Physical				
a. Blood temperature	______	______	______	______
b. Arterial blood pressure	______	______	______	______
c. Venous blood pressure	______	______	______	______
2. Chemical				
a. $PaCO_2$ + arterial H^+	______	______	______	______
b. $PaCO_2$	______	______	______	______
B. Neural				
1. Impulse from higher brain centres	______	______	______	______
2. Inflation or deflation of lungs	______	______	______	______
3. Limb Movement	______	______	______	______

Self-Test

1. Directions: Indicate how each of the following factors directly affects cardiac output by placing an increase ($\uparrow$), decrease ($\downarrow$) or no change ($\leftrightarrow$) symbol in each space.

Factor	HR	x	SV	=	$\dot{Q}$
a. Increased intraventricular pressure	_____		_____		_____
b. Increased parasympathetic nerve stimulation	_____		_____		_____
c. Increased sympathetic nerve stimulation	_____		_____		_____
d. Smaller respiratory movements	_____		_____		_____
e. Increased plasma epinephrine	_____		_____		_____

2. Which of the following are good examples of neural stimuli?

   1. changes in body temperature
   2. changes in arterial blood PO_2 and PCO_2
   3. changes in arterial blood H+
   4. changes in the rate of impulse transmission from the stretch receptors in muscle or joints

   A = 1,2,3; B = 1,3; C = 2,4; D = 4; E = 1,2,3 & 4.

3. The action of humoral or neural agents on the cardiorespiratory centres can be categorized into a central (direct) or reflex (indirect) action. Which of the following stimuli are considered to have a direct action on the cardiorespiratory centres?

   1. increased blood temperature
   2. increased arterial blood carbon dioxide tension
   3. impulse transmission from higher brain centres
   4. increased arterial blood pressure

   A = 1,2,3; B = 1,3; C = 2,4; D = 4; E = 1,2,3 & 4.

Answers to Self-Test of Module 11 - Cardiorespiratory Control

1.	HR	x	Sv	=	Q
a.	↔		↑		↑
b.	↓		↔		↓
c.	↑		↑		↑
d.	↔		↓		↓
e.	↑		↑		↑

2. D = 4

3. A = 1,2,3

SECTION 3

CARDIORESPIRATORY CONSIDERATIONS

Self Test

1. The change in intrapleural pressure from -4 mm Hg to -8 mm Hg during inspiration is due to the

    a. compression of the abdomen
    b. pumping action of the larynx
    c. compression of the thoracic cage
    d. expansion of the thoracic cage
    e. more than one of the above

2. The total of tidal volume plus inspiratory reserve volume is named:

    a. vital capacity
    b. inspiratory volume
    c. inspiratory capacity
    d. functional reserve capacity
    e. expiratory reserve capacity

3. The largest percentage of carbon dioxide carried in the blood is carried as

    a. dissolved carbon dioxide
    b. a chemical combination with water to form carbonic acid and then biocarbonate
    c. a chemical combination with hemoglobin to form a carbonic compound
    d. a chemical combination with carbonic anhydrase to form water
    e. none of the above.

4. A volume of dry air at 760 mm Hg barometric pressure is found to contain 5% carbon dioxide by volume. The partial pressure of the carbon dioxide mixture would be:

    a. 30 mm Hg
    b. 34 mm Hg
    c. 38 mm Hg
    d. 42 mm Hg
    e. 46 mm Hg

5. The following question is to be answered with reference to the following data: $\dot{V}_E$ = 20 litres/min. (STPD), F_{ECO_2} = 0.04

Calculate rate of CO_2 production ($\dot{V}_{CO_2}$)

a. 250 ml/min.
b. 240 ml/min.
c. 800 ml/min.
d. 1000 ml/min.
e. 1200 ml/min.

6. What is the content of oxygen in blood 100% saturated with oxygen, given that the hemoglobin concentration is 12 grams/100 ml. of blood?

a. 20 vol%
b. 18 vol%
c. 16 vol%
d. 14 vol%
e. 12 vol%

7. A man working on a bicycle ergometer with a cardiac output of 10 litres/min and a blood pressure reading of 160 systolic and 100 diastolic would have a total peripheral resistance of

a. 0.08 mm Hg/Litre/min
b. 8.0 mm Hg/Litre/min
c. 12.0 mm Hg/Litre/min
d. 14.0 mm Hg/Litre/min
e. 120 mm Hg/Litre/min

8. Two resting subjects with no structural heart disease have the same oxygen consumption per minute.

	Systemic arterial oxygen content	Pulmonary arterial oxygen content
Subject I	200 ml/1	160 ml/1
Subject II	80 ml/1	60 ml/1

Compared with that of Subject II, the cardiac output of Subject I is:

a. half as large
b. three-fourths as large
c. the same
d. 1.25 times as large
e. twice as large

9. In skeletal muscle, the increased oxygen uptake during strenuous exercise is met by:

a. increasing blood flow to the muscles
b. increasing capillary surface area
c. decreasing the affinity of oxygen for hemoglobin
d. all of the above are correct
e. only a. and b. are correct

10. A good example of a negative feedback mechanism which operates in the control of the cardiorespiratory systems is demonstrated by:

a. an increased arterial pressure above normal rest values of about 100 mm.Hg which will cause a decrease in heart rate, stroke volume and resistance to blood flow which in turn lowers arterial blood pressure back to normal resting levels.

b. a decreased arterial blood pressure below normal resting values of about 180 mm.Hg which in turn cause a decrease in heart rate, stroke volume, and resistance to blood flow which in turn raises arterial blood pressure back to normal resting values

c. a decrease in arterial P_{O_2} below rest values which will cause hypoventilation which will in turn raise the P_{O_2} in the arterial blood back to normal values.

d. an increased arterial P_{CO_2} above normal values seen at rest which will stimulate the central chemoreceptors to decrease minute ventilation which will result in a lowering of the arterial P_{CO_2} back to normal resting values.

e. an increased arterial pH which stimulates the central chemoreceptors to increase ventilation which in turn results in the arterial pH returning to normal resting values.

Answers to Self-Test on SECTION 3 - CARDIORESPIRATORY CONSIDERATIONS

1. d
2. c
3. b
4. c
5. c
6. c
7. c
8. a
9. d
10. a

SECTION 4

PHYSICAL TRAINING

Module 12

INTERVAL TRAINING AND OTHER CONDITIONING METHODS

Module 13

PHYSIOLOGICAL EFFECTS OF PHYSICAL TRAINING

Module 12

INTERVAL TRAINING AND OTHER CONDITIONING METHODS

Objectives

Upon completion of this module the student will be able to:

1. List three considerations important to all training programs.
2. List and describe the three principles of training.
3. Determine the predominant energy system for a specific event and demonstrate this ability by completing a table such as Table 12-1 p. 241 in Mathews and Fox.
4. Describe the main phases of a training program and give specific examples of activities in each phase.
5. Explain why intermittent work (interval training) is useful in improving all three energy systems.
6. Describe the level of energy production and fatigue during intermittent work of various types.
7. Describe why fatigue is reduced in intermittent work compared with continuous work (total work equated).
8. Develop a training prescription in terms of its frequency, duration and intensity or its repetitions, distance, time and relief interval. (see Table 12-7 p. 258 Mathews and Fox).
9. Describe the five variables which can be changed to fulfil the overload principle.
10. Describe a training program designed to stress the aerobic or anaerobic systems.
11. Outline on what the time and type of relief interval depends in an interval training program.
12. Define interval training terms.
13. Write a training prescription using tables such as Table 12-8 or 12-9 pp. 262-263 in Mathews and Fox for the improvement of specific energy systems.
14. Outline and list other major conditioning programs and their uses.

Reading Assignment

Chapter 12, pp. 239-270.

Exercises

Part I

1. Without looking at Table 12-1 complete the following table. Check your answers against Table 12-1 & 2, pp. 241-242 of Mathews and Fox.

Event	Approx. Time of Performance (min:sec)	Speed (ATP-CP Strength)	Aerobic Capacity	Anaerobic Capacity
100 yds.	0:12	______	______	______
440 yds.	1:15	______	______	______
1 mile	4:30	______	______	______
6 miles	35:00	______	______	______
Marathon	150:00	______	______	______
baseball	______	______	______	______
tennis	______	______	______	______

2. Diagram the changes in the ATP-CP stores as a subject exercises in intermittent work.

Part II

1. A very quick way to judge the intensity of training is to count the ________________________ at the end of the exercise.

2. The ________________ ______________________ can be counted for ____________ seconds and multiplied by _____________ to obtain a value for 1 minute.

3. Target heart rates may be obtained by taking the value 210 minus a subject's __________________________.

4. Another method of controlling training intensity is based upon the rule that the times for training distances between 55 and 220 yds. should be between ____________ and ____________ seconds slower, respectively, than the _______________ times for those distances measured from a running start. See Table 12-5 Mathews and Fox for complete program.

5. Develop a training program as in Table 12-7 for 1 event with which you are familiar.

Self-Test

1. In order to observe an improvement in performance following a program of training which of the following are considered important?

   1. training should be specific to the event

   2. training need not place an overload on the predominant energy sources needed for the event

   3. training should overload the specific energy sources needed for the event

   4. for the best training effects, it is not necessary to train specifically for the event

   A = 1,2,3; B = 1,3; C = 2,4; D = 4; E = 1,2,3 & 4.

2. A young athlete was observed to have a low capacity in ATP-CP reservoir. In order to possibly improve this energy source system, it would be best to place him on a training program in which he

   a. jogged slowly at least 5 miles per day
   b. ran as fast as possible for a distance of 50 yards once each day
   c. ran as fast as he could 2 miles each day
   d. ran as fast as he could about 100 yards at least 6 times a day with a 30 second rest between each run
   e. ran as fast as he could 400 yards with 10 second rest between each of 3 trials

3. In intermittent training compared to continuous training there will be

   a. more lactic acid produced
   b. less lactic acid produced
   c. more energy produced by the ATP-CP energy source and less by the lactic acid system
   d. less energy produced by the ATP-CP system and more by the lactic acid system
   e. none of the above

4. Specifically, in regard to the development of the energy systems, intermittent work or the interval training system accomplishes the following

   1. It allows the ATP-CP system to be used over and over. This, in turn, provides an adequate stimulus for promoting an increase in the energy capacity of this system and aids in delaying the onset of fatigue by not delving so deeply into the lactic acid system.

   2. With proper regulation of the duration and type of relief interval, the involvement of the lactic acid system will be maximal and thus improved.

   3. By working long enough at a sufficient intensity and by improvement in the maximal attainable stroke volume, the aerobic system is developed.

   4. It allows the lactic acid system to be used over and over. This, in turn, provides an adequate stimulus for promoting an increase in the energy capacity of this system and aids in delaying the onset of fatigue by not stressing too severely the ATP-CP system.

   A = 1,2,3; B = 1,3; C = 2,4; D = 4; E = 1,2,3 & 4.

Answers to Self-Test on Module 12 - Interval Training and Other Conditioning Methods

1. B = 1,3
2. d
3. c
4. A = 1,2,3.

Module 13

PHYSIOLOGICAL EFFECTS OF PHYSICAL TRAINING

Objectives

Upon completion of this module the student will be able to:

1. Identify the three major areas in which aerobic adaptation to training occurs in the skeletal muscle.
2. Describe the changes which take place in each of the major areas of aerobic adaptation, which occurs in skeletal muscle.
3. List the two major anaerobic adaptations that occur in skeletal muscle as a result of training.
4. Describe the changes which take place in the skeletal muscle which contribute to the two major anaerobic adaptations.
5. Describe the relative changes in red and white muscle fibres as a result of training.
6. Complete a table showing the changes at the musclular level which occur due to training.
   See Table 13-1 p. 277 Mathews and Fox for an example table.
7. Describe the changes in cardiorespiratory (systemic) capacities as a result of training at rest, during submaximal exercise and maximal exercise.
8. Complete a table showing systemic changes which result from training. For an example see the summary on p. 309 of Mathews and Fox.
9. Describe changes which occur in body composition, blood pressure, heat acclimatization, and respiratory system as a result of training.
10. List and describe the factors which influence training as shown on p. 253 of Mathews and Fox.
11. Describe the effects on training of genetic factors, and the mode of exercise, and be able to describe the factors which maintain the training effect.

Reading Assignment

Chapter 13, pp. 271-315

Exercises

Part I

Directions: Complete the following table with arrows showing changes with training:

↑ (increase); ↓ (decrease); ↔ (no change); X (no information needed)

Variable	Rest	Submaximal Exercise	Maximal Exercise
Heart Rate			
Stroke volume			
Cardiac Output			
a-v O_2 difference			
lactic acid	X		
muscle blood flow	X		
blood volume			
capillary-fibre ratio		X	X
vagal tone		X	X
parasympathetic tone			

Self-Test

1. Which of the following factors influence the degree of training which results from a program of exercise?

   1. Intensity of the training sessions

   2. The frequency per week of the training sessions

   3. The duration of the training program

   4. The type of training program i.e. the specificity of training effects.

   A = 1,2,3; B = 1,3; C = 2,4; D = 4; E = 1,2,3 & 4

The following paired statements describe two entities that are to be compared in a quantitative sense.

Answer: A if a. is greater than b.
B if b. is greater than a.
C if the two are equal or very nearly equal

2. a. Increase in maximal oxygen uptake after training on a treadmill and being tested on a treadmill.

   b. Increase in maximal oxygen uptake after training on a treadmill and being tested on a bicycle ergometer.

3. a. Increase in maximal oxygen uptake after training on a bicycle and being tested on a treadmill.

   b. Increase in maximal oxygen uptake after training on a bicycle and being tested on a bicycle ergometer.

4. a. Increase in stroke volume measured in the trained limb when training is conducted in arms or legs only.

   b. Increase in stroke volume measured in the untrained limb when training is conducted in arms or legs only.

5. a. Decrease in lactic acid accumulation following sprint training measured during submaximal work.

   b. Decrease in lactic acid accumulation following endurance training measured during submaximal exercise.

Answers to Self-Test on Module 13 - Physiological Effects of Physical Training

1. E = 1,2,3 & 4
2. A
3. B
4. A
5. B

Self-Test

1. In developing a training program to improve athletic performance which of the following considerations are appropriate?

    1. Analysis of the athletic performance to estimate the predominant energy sources involved

    2. the training program should be specific to developing the energy systems predominantly used during the athletic performance

    3. the training program be as specific as possible in the musculature trained and the neuromuscular pattern used

    4. the training program be gradually increased in intensity in conformity with the overload principle

    A = 1,2,3; B = 1,3; C = 2,4; D = 4; E = 1,2,3 & 4.

2. In interval training compared with continuous training

    1. more energy is produced by the ATP-PC system and less by the lactic acid system

    2. at a given intensity more work can be performed before the fatigue associated lactic acid accumulation

    3. the ATP-PC energy capacity may be improved by the stimulus of repeated use of this system.

    4. the higher stroke volume during the relief interval may provide an overload stimulus resulting in improvement of the aerobic system.

    A = 1,2,3; B = 1,3; C = 2,4; D = 4; E = 1,2,3 & 4.

3. Which of the following statements appear valid?

1. to achieve a training effect one must exercise at an intensity which produces a heart rate of at least 135 beats/min.

2. the gains in $\dot{V}O_2$ max with training are directly related to initial fitness level

3. training improves the heart muscle (central) but has little effect on the muscle biochemistry

4. a running program results in a more general improvement than a cycling program

A = 1,2,3; B = 1,3; C = 2,4; D = 4; E = 1,2,3 & 4.

4. A young athlete was observed to have a low capacity of energy yield from the lactic acid system. In order to improve this energy source it would be best to place him on a training program in which he performs:

a. a number of repetitions and sets of a work to relief interval of 3 minutes: 3 minutes with a "rest relief"
b. a number of repetitions and sets of a work to relief interval of 1 minute: 3 minutes with a "work relief"
c. a number of repetitions and sets of a work to relief interval of 1 minute: 1/2 minute with a "work relief"
d. a continuous run as fast as possible for approximately 2 miles
e. a number of repetitions and sets of a work to relief interval of 1 minute: 1/2 minute with a "rest relief".

5. Which of the following is true?

a. Long slow distance (LSD) training develops mainly the anaerobic energy systems.
b. In a sprint training regimen the relief period should be short to avoid complete recovery of the ATP-PC system.
c. Interval sprinting may be used to develop the aerobic system as well as some development of the anaerobic energy systems.
d. Football players should train their aerobic system since a player may be on the field 20 to 40 minutes during a game.
e. Competitive cross-country skiers should emphasize the anaerobic system in their training program.

6. Which of the following physiological adaptations may result from a period of physical training of both aerobic and anaerobic energy sources?

1. an increased glycogen storage and an increased phosphagen storage

2. an increased rate of carbohydrate oxidation as well as fat oxidation

3. an increased myoglobin content

4. decreased blood cholesterol and triglyceride levels and a decreased lean body mass.

A = 1,2,3; B = 1,3; C = 2,4; D = 4; E = 1,2,3 & 4.

7. Endurance trained athletes compared to sedentary subjects exhibit:

1. a greater blood flow to active muscles at a given submaximal workload

2. a lower lactic acid production when comparing both groups working at 60% of their VO_2 max.

3. a lesser sweat production and sweat which is less hypotonic

4. in maximum exercise a greater $a\text{-}\bar{v}O_2$ difference.

A = 1,2,3; B = 1,3; C = 2,4; D = 4; E = 1,2,3 & 4.

8. Endurance trained athletes compared to sedentary subjects exhibit:

1. higher maximal heart rates

2. similar heart size (left ventricular cavity) but thicker myocardial walls

3. a much larger cardiac output in both submaximal and maximal exercise

4. a resting and submaximal exercise bradycardia.

A = 1,2,3; B = 1,3; C = 2,4; D = 4; E = 1,2,3 & 4.

9. With regard to factors influencing the training response which of the following statement(s) is/are valid?

1. the training intensity should be expressed relative to the subject's $\dot{V}O_2$ max.

2. for an individual with resting heart rate of 70 beats/min and maximum heart rate of 170 beats/min, to achieve a training threshold a heart rate of 130 beats/min would be prescribed

3. training adaptations have a specificity related to the type or mode of training, the muscle groups and fibre types employed, and the energy system stressed

4. following 12 weeks of endurance training the increased VO_2 max can be maintained by as little as one training session per week.

A = 1,2,3; B = 1,3; C = 2,4; D = 4; E = 1,2,3 & 4.

Answers to Self-Test on SECTION 4 - PHYSICAL TRAINING

1. E = 1,2,3 & 4
2. E = 1,2,3 & 4
3. D = 4
4. b
5. c
6. A = 1,2,3
7. C = 2,4
8. D = 4
9. A = 1,2,3

SECTION 5

ENVIRONMENTAL ASPECTS

Module 14

DIFFUSION, OSMOSIS, AND DROWNING

Module 15

EXERCISE AND ACID-BASE BALANCE

Module 16

SCUBA AND PERFORMANCE AT ALTITUDE

Module 17

HEAT BALANCE: PREVENTION OF HEAT STROKE IN ATHLETICS

Module 14

DIFFUSION, OSMOSIS, AND DROWNING

Objectives

Upon completion of this module the student will be able to:

1. Describe cellular exchange by

   a. diffusion and facilitated diffusion
   b. osmosis with understanding of isotonic, hypertonic and hypotonic
   c. electrical forces
   d. active transport with the sodium-potassium pump.

2. As an example of cellular equilibrium, describe the physiological consequences of (a) freshwater drowning (b) sea water drowning.

Reading Assignment

Chapter 14, pp. 319-331.

Exercises

Answer the objectives

Self-Test

1. Food moves from the blood through the ____________________ and into the ________ and waste material from the cell outward. Oxygen moves into the cell by ______________ since there is a greater concentration of O_2 in the capillary than in the cell. Similarly there is an opposite diffusion _______________ for CO_2. Glucose moves into the cell by combining with a carrier substance, thus this process is called _______________ diffusion. Some particles are too large to pass through the cell membrane pores. If these particles are in equal amount on both sides of the membrane the solutions on the two sides are said to be ______________ to each other. If on the inside of the cell membrane there are more molecules than on the outside, water molecules will diffuse _________ the cell. The solution on the outside of the cell is termed ________________ to the inside of the cell.

2. Name the ions which are most concentrated outside the cell and those most concentrated inside the cell. What keeps sodium in higher concentration outside the cell?

3. In freshwater drowning the water swallowed is ______________ to the blood, thus water passes into the bloodstream by ____________. The diluted blood is ______________ to the red blood cells and therefore water passes into the red blood cells. The bursting of these red blood cells is called ________________.

4. In sea water drowning the water is ________________ to blood thus water moves from the blood to the _________. The loss of blood water makes the blood __________________ to the red blood cells and water leaves the red blood cells causing them to shrink.

Answers to Self-Test on Module 14 - Diffusion, Osmosis, and Drowning

1. interstitial fluid
   cell
   diffusion
   gradient
   facilitated diffusion
   isotonic
   into
   hypotonic

2. sodium, calcium, chloride (outside);potassium, magnesium, phosphate (inside);active transport-sodium potassium pump

3. hypotonic
   osmosis
   hypotonic
   hemolysis

4. hypertonic
   lungs
   hypertonic

Module 15

EXERCISE AND ACID-BASE BALANCE

Objectives

Upon completion of this module the student will be able to:

1. Define the terms acid and base, the constituents of a buffer system and the meaning of the term pH.
2. Describe the role of minute ventilation in the control of pH in the body.
3. Define alkali reserve.
4. Describe the role of the kidney in the regulation of body acid-base balance.
5. Describe the effect of exercise on the acid-base balance and the three main factors which determine the amount of acid produced in exercise.
6. State the values for normal resting pH, and plasma bicarbonate and values found following strenuous exercise.
7. Illustrate the relationship between blood lactate concentration and blood pH. See Figure 15-2.

Reading Assignment

Chapter 15, pp. 332-338.

Self-Test

1. The lowest urinary pH which is reached in extreme acidosis is

   a. 7.4
   b. 8.6
   c. 7.0
   d. 6.0
   e. 4.5

2. An acid is a chemical compound which in solution

   a. gives up hydroxyl ions
   b. gives up (OH^-)
   c. accepts (H^+)
   d. gives up (H^+)
   e. none of the above.

Answers to Self-Test on Module 15 - Exercise and Acid-Base Balance

1. e
2. d

Module 16

SCUBA AND PERFORMANCE AT ALTITUDE

Objectives

Upon completion of this module the student will be able to:

1. Describe how the volume of gas is related to pressure and temperature. Write an equation to describe the relationships.
2. Describe how a diver may suffer air embolism.
3. Describe spontaneous pneumothorax.
4. Identify the causes of the bends and how they can be avoided.
5. Define oxygen poisoning.
6. Describe the pressure changes which cause (a) squeeze (b) aerotitis.
7. a) Outline the physiological considerations that would lead one to expect a reduction in endurance capacity at altitudes above 5,000 feet. b) Describe the rate of reduction in endurance capacity ($\dot{V}O_2$ max) as one assends above 5,000 feet.
8. Describe the physiological changes which occur with acclimatization to altitude.
9. Identify the advantages that may be gained by training at altitude. Identify the major problems of hard training at altitude.
10. Discuss how training at altitude affects performance at altitude and at sea level.

Reading Assignment

Chapter 16, pp. 339-361.

Exercises

1. Describe the events which may lead to air embolism, pneumothorax and the bends.

2. Why should goggles not be worn for diving?

3. At altitude the barometric pressure was 700 mmHg. At sea level the barometric pressure was 760 mmHg. In both cases calculate the oxygen pressure or tension.

4. List the major physiological changes which occur during acclimatization to altitude.

5. Does training at altitude improve sea level performance of non-athletes? of athletes?

Self-Test

1. What is the atmospheric pressure 66 feet under water?

   a. 1 atmosphere
   b. 2 atmospheres
   c. 3 atmospheres
   d. 4 atmospheres
   e. 29.4 psi

2. If a diver inhaled 2 l of gas at 33 feet under water what would be the volume of this gas in the lungs when he surfaced with his breath held?

   a. 4 l
   b. 2.5 l
   c. 6 l
   d. 2 l
   e. 3 l

3. Which of the following events contribute to oxygen poisoning?

   1. breathing 100% oxygen at the pressures below the surface forces oxygen into solution with the blood

   2. the oxygen in red blood cells is not removed and therefore carbon dioxide cannot be taken up from the tissues

   3. the excess CO_2 and O_2 in tissues disturbs cerebral blood flow

   4. too much O_2 in the red blood cells results in hemolysis

   A = 1,2,3; B = 1,3; C = 2,4; D = 4; E = 1,2,3 & 4.

4. An individual has a $\dot{V}O_2$ max of 50 ml/kg·min. What would be his approximate aerobic capacity measured at 10,000 feet altitude?

   a. 50 ml/kg·min.
   b. 57 ml/kg·min.
   c. 35 ml/kg·min.
   d. 42 ml/kg·min.
   e. 38 ml/kg·min.

5. Performance of athletic events at altitude

   1. is diminished for primarily anaerobic events

   2. is not greatly altered for anaerobic events

   3. is not greatly altered for aerobic events

   4. is diminished for events of an aerobic nature

   A = 1,2,3; B = 1,3; C = 2,4; D = 4; E = 1,2,3 & 4.

Answers to Self-Test on Module 16 - Scuba and Performance at Altitude

1. c
2. a
3. A = 1,2,3
4. d
5. C = 2,4

Module 17

HEAT BALANCE: PREVENTION OF HEAT STROKE IN ATHLETICS

Objectives

Upon completion of this module the student will be able to:

1. Outline the sequential physiological events that occur during heat stroke.
2. Describe four ways by which body heat may be dissipated.
3. Estimate how much heat is produced by the body under resting and exercise conditions.
4. Outline two ways in which heat (or cold) is sensed by the body.
5. Outline the effector organ responses to cold and heat.
6. Outline how the thermoregulatory centre maintains a relatively constant temperature. Is the reference temperature changed in exercise?
7. State the principal means of heat loss during exercise.
8. State the major circulatory demands when exercising in a hot, humid environment.
9. Explain how salt and water depletion during exercise can lead to serious heat disorders.
10. Outline correct methods for salt and water supplementation in athletes working in hot, humid environments.
11. Outline reasons to explain the particular heat problem in football.
12. Describe heat acclimatization and outline the importance of physical conditioning in heat acclimatization.
13. Outline considerations for the prevention of heat illnesses and emergency procedures should heat problems occur.
14. Describe physiological responses to cold.

Reading Assignment

Chapter 17, pp. 362-388.

Exercises

1. Outline the sequence of physiological events resulting in body temperatures in excess of 40°C when exercising in a hot humid environment.

2. Outline a program of salt and water replacement for athletes working in the heat.

3. Diagram the weather guide that may be used to estimate severity of climatic conditions.

Self-Test

1. An 80kg athlete consumes 2 l of oxygen per minute for the duration of a 15 minute run. Assuming an R of 0.82 calculate how much heat the body must dissipate so that body temperature does not go above 38°C.

   1. 78.2 kcal
   2. 144.9 kcal
   3. 1.18°C
   4. 8.73°C

   A = 1,2,3; B = 1,3; C = 2,4; D = 4; E = 1,2,3 & 4.

2. Acclimatization to exercise in the heat results in

   1. an earlier onset of the sweating response and greater sweat rates
   2. an increased blood volume
   3. a decreased loss of salt in sweat
   4. a cutaneous vasoconstriction to restrict skin blood flow

   A = 1,2,3; B = 1,3; C = 2,4; D = 4; E = 1,2,3 & 4.

Answers to Self-Test on Module 17 - Heat Balance: Prevention of Heat Stroke in Athletics

1. B = 1,3
2. A = 1,2,3

Self-Test

1. Sodium ions are predominantly found outside the cell because:

   a. the cell membrane is completely impermeable to sodium
   b. they combine with the CO_2 diffusing out of the cell to produce sodium carbo-oxide
   c. the electrochemical force tends to drive sodium out of the cell
   d. the interior of the cell is hypertonic to the interstitial fluid and sodium is driven out of the cell by osmosis
   e. the so-called sodium-potassium pump transports sodium out of the cell.

2. Steps in the sequence of fresh water and sea water drowning are shown in columns below. In which case or cases are both statements correct?

FRESH WATER DROWNING	SEA WATER DROWNING
1. water taken into the alveoli is hypertonic to blood	1. water taken into the alveoli is hypotonic to blood
2. the red blood cell undergoes hemolysis	2. the red blood cell shrinks (plasmolysis)
3. the lungs on autopsy would be full of water	3. the lungs on autopsy would contain no water
4. low O_2 concentration and electrolyte disturbance results in ventricular fibrillation	4. filling of the lungs with blood water leads to pulmonary edema and a drop in blood pressure

A = 1,2,3; B = 1,3; C = 2,4; D = 4; E = 1,2,3 & 4.

3. According to the gas laws (Boyle's Law and Charles' Law):

1. with a change of temperature (T_1 to T_2) the final volume (V_2) of a gas is related to the initial volume (V_1) as
$$V_2 = V_1 \times \frac{T_1}{T_2}$$

2. with a change of pressure (P_1 to P_2) the final volume V_2 of a gas is related to the initial volume (V_1) as
$$V_2 = V_1 \times \frac{P_1}{P_2}$$

3. the volume of gas is inversely related to the temperature of the gas

4. the volume of a gas is inversely related to the pressure on the gas

A = 1,2,3; B = 1,3; C = 2,4; D = 4; E = 1,2,3 & 4.

4. A volume of gas measured 3 1 at the water surface level. Under 66' of fresh water what is the approximate gas volume? (Do not account for any temperature change effects)

a. 3 1
b. 9 1
c. 1 1
d. 2 1
e. 4½ 1

5. A scuba diver inflates his lungs with 3 1 of gas at a depth of 33'. The diver holds his breath during slow ascent. Which of the following possibilities are true?

1. the diver may get air embolism

2. the diver may get "squeeze"

3. the diver may get spontaneous pneumothorax

4. the diver may get the "bends"

A = 1,2,3; B = 1,3; C = 2,4; D = 4; E = 1,2,3 & 4.

6. An individual has a $\dot{V}O_2$ max test at sea level with a resultant $\dot{V}O_2$ max of 70 ml/kg.min. He then goes to the old site of the Mexico Olympics (altitude 7,000 feet). On the fifth day his $\dot{V}O_2$ max was measured. What result would you expect ($\dot{V}O_2$ max in ml/kg.min)?

a. 48
b. 65
c. 76
d. 70
e. 57

7. Which of the following may occur during the process of acclimatization to altitude with combined physical training?

1. mountain (altitude) sickness

2. increased haemoglobin concentration

3. elimination of bicarbonate in the urine

4. increased minute ventilation

A = 1,2,3; B = 1,3; C = 2,4; D = 4; E = 1,2,3 & 4.

8. Specific heat:

1. is the heat required to effect a given temperature change per unit mass of substance

2. is the heat required to raise the temperature of 1 kg of water $1^{o}C$.

3. of the body is 0.83 kcal/kg/^{o}C

4. of water is 0.83 kcal/kg/^{o}C

A = 1,2,3; B = 1,3; C = 2,4; D = 4; E = 1,2,3 & 4.

9. In temperature regulation, which of the following are correct?

1. in response to cold, body heat may be preserved by shivering and cutaneous vasoconstriction

2. in response to cold, increased thyroxin and nor-epinephrine output result in increased body heat production

3. in exercise the set point or reference temperature of the thermoregulatory centre is higher than in rest

4. free nerve endings in the skin are the receptors for environmental temperature changes

A = 1,2,3; B = 1,3; C = 2,4; D = 4; E = 1,2,3 & 4.

10. Concerning exercise in the heat, which of the following is/are true?

1. there is an extra circulatory stress due to cutaneous vasoconstriction resulting in increased peripheral resistance

2. in temperatures above 80°F the weather guide suggests heat stroke as a risk and football practice should be conducted in light dress only

3. since sweat is hypotonic, large sweat loss may, through a sequence of events, result in an increased blood volume

4. long duration exercise may be limited by hyperthermia

A = 1,2,3; B = 1,3; C = 2,4; D = 4; E = 1,2,3 & 4.

11. An 80 kg man performed steady state exercise for 2 hours at an average oxygen consumption of 2 l/min. The R was 1.0. Therefore total heat production was calculated to be approximately 1200 kcal. Calculate the approximate required heat loss so body temperature was 40°C at the end of the exercise. (Resting body temperature 37°C; body specific heat 0.83 kcal/kg/°C.)

a. 18 kcal.
b. 1200 kcal.
c. 950 kcal.
d. 2100 kcal.
e. 1000 kcal.

12. Immediately following strenuous exercise of short duration the blood pH, lactate levels and plasma bicarbonate concentration levels would be approximated best by

	pH	Lactate mg%	Bicarbonate mM/L
a.	8.0	120	32
b.	7.0	42	18
c.	7.0	120	18
d.	7.6	100	28
e.	6.5	190	1

Answers on Self-Test on SECTION 5 - ENVIRONMENTAL ASPECTS

1. e
2. C = 2,4
3. C = 2,4
4. c
5. B = 1,3
6. b
7. E = 1,2,3 & 4
8. B = 1,3
9. E = 1,2,3 & 4
10. D = 4
11. e
12. c

SECTION 6

NUTRITION AND BODY COMPOSITION

Module 18

NUTRITION, ATHLETIC PERFORMANCE, AND OBESITY

Module 19

SOMATOTYPE AND BODY FAT

Module 18

NUTRITION, ATHLETIC PERFORMANCE AND OBESITY

Objectives

Upon completion of this module the student will be able to:

1. Define positive and negative energy balance.
2. Give examples of fats and distinguish between saturated and unsaturated fats. Give examples of carbohydrates.
3. Identify the structure of proteins and the importance of protein in the diet.
4. Describe the percent contribution of protein, fat and carbohydrate which make up a recommended diet.
5. Describe recommended times for food and liquid consumption prior to competition.
6. In compeititions of long duration, especially in the heat, identify the liquid supplement that should be used, why it should be used, and how much should be used.
7. Describe the special considerations for a diet following activity.
8. Describe the diet which seems most beneficial in preparation for athletic performance.
9. Describe how muscle glycogen can be increased in preparation for endurance events.
10. Name the diseases to which obesity is related.
11. Define obesity.
12. Describe evidence that suggests prevention of obesity is particularly important during pre-adolescence.

Reading Assignment

Chapter 18, pp. 391-410.

Exercises

1. Outline the normal food requirements in kcal for an 18-22 year old male and female. What per cent should be protein, fat, carbohydrate?

2. Outline the food requirements for the boy and girl in the above example if the boy played one hour of basketball every other day and the girl did one hour of gymnastics every other day.

3. What suggestions would you make for a precompetition meal?

4. How might diet be altered to favorably influence endurance performance?

5. What is adipocyte hyperplasia?

Self-Test

1. An 18 year old male cycles at 13 mph for one-half hour daily. What should his dietary intake be to maintain energy balance?

   a. $2000 + 333 + (333 \times \frac{1}{10}) = 2366$ kcal

   b. $2800 + 333 + (333 \times \frac{1}{10}) = 3166$ kcal

   c. $5450 + (5450 \times \frac{1}{10}) = 5995$ kcal

   d. 2800 kcal

   e. 333 kcal.

2. To build muscle glycogen stores in preparation for endurance competition one should incorporate which of the following suggestions?

   1. eat primarily a carbohydrate diet in the week before competition.

   2. exhaust the muscles of glycogen by heavy exercise one week before competition followed for three days by a low carbohydrate diet.

   3. decrease water intake in the three days prior to competition then drink as much as possible on the day of competition.

   4. in the three days prior to competition add large amounts of carbohydrate to the diet.

   A = 1,2,3; B = 1,3; C = 2,4; D = 4; E = 1,2,3 & 4.

3 Obesity

1. can be defined as a weight 25% above normal body weight of a 25 year old

2. results from a combination of the number of adipocytes and their lipid content

3. is related to diabetes and coronary heart disease

4. may result at least in part from lack of exercise during pre-adolescent years.

A = 1,2,3; B = 1,3; C = 2,4; D = 4; E = 1,2,3 & 4.

Answers to Self-Test on Module 18 - Nutrition, Athletic Performance and Obesity

1. b
2. C = 2,4
3. E = 1,2,3 & 4

Module 19

SOMATOTYPE AND
BODY FAT

Objectives

Upon completion of this module the student will be able to:

1. Define endomorphy, mesomorphy and ectomorphy.
2. Describe how the Sheldon Somatotype is used to develop a profile of body type and be able to give the appropriate numerical identification for each of the 3 body classifications.
3. Describe the technique developed by Heath-Carter to obtain a somatotype and suitable scores for various types of athletes. Calculate the ponderal index given the subjects height and weight.
4. Describe the ways excess fat stored on the body reduces the capacity for physical performance.
5. Define specific gravity of a body.
6. Define density of a body.
7. Describe Archimedes' Principle.
8. Calculate density and specific gravity of an object given the appropriate necessary information.
9. Describe how the density of a human body may be calculated by the underwater weighing technique.
10. Describe how per cent fat is calculated.
11. Calculate the per cent fat of a human body given the appropriate measurements of weight in air, weight in water, density of water at a given temperature, the residual volume or vital capacity, and the appropriate formula to calculate per cent fat from body density.
12. Calculate body fat using the Sloan-Weir Nomogram for predicting body density.
13. Describe problems which might result from too much weight loss.
14. Describe the Iowa technique for predicting minimal weight values.
15. Calculate minimal weight values given appropriate measurements.

Reading Assignment

Chapter 19, pp. 411-433

Exercises

1. Calculate the ponderal index of a subject who was 68 inches tall and 130 lbs. To solve the answer use Figure 19-4 - your answer should be 13.4.

2. Calculate the density of an object with Mass = 100 gms. and
Volume = 10 cc.

3. If an object weighed 50 kgms in air and only 10 kgms in water, what is its specific gravity?

4. Calculate the body density of the following subject

   Ht. = 70 in.
   Wt. in air = 70 kg or 70,000 gm
   Wt. in water = 2 kg or 2000 gm
   Density of water at temperature measured = .9950 gm/cc
   Vital Capacity (BTPS) = 5000 cc
   Residual Volume = 0.24 x V.C. = 0.24 x 5000 cc = 1200 cc

   For your answer see the example on page 424 of Mathews and Fox.

5. Calculate the minimal weight of a young wrestler using the Iowa study formulae (both long and short forms).

   Wt. = 160 lbs.
   Ht. = 72 in.
   Chest diameter = 26 cm
   Chest depth = 20 cm
   Bitrochanteric diameter = 30 cm
   Bi-iliac diameter = 24 cm
   Wrist diameter (sum of both wrists) = 6 cm
   Ankle diameter (sum of both ankles) = 16 cm

   See page 431 of Mathews and Fox for an example.

Self-Test

1. What is the approximate per cent fat of a man with the following measurements?

   Ht. = 180 cm
   Wt. in air = 80 kg and wt. in water = 3.00 kg.
   Density of water = 0.9960 gm/cc
   V.C. (BTPS) = 6000 cc

   Note: $\text{per cent fat} = \left(\frac{4.570}{\text{body density}} - 4.142\right) \times 100$

   a. 30%
   b. 11%
   c. 16%
   d. 19%
   e. 24%

2. Calculate the ponderal index of a woman given that she is 68 in. tall and weighs 125 lbs.

   a. 12
   b. 15
   c. 9
   d. 10
   e. 14

3. The predominant characteristic(s) of ectomorphy is (are):

   1. linearity
   2. muscular
   3. thin muscles
   4. softness of body

   A = 1,2,3; B = 1,3; C = 2,4; D = 4; E = 1,2,3 & 4.

4. An object weighed 90 kg in air and 30 kg in water. What is its specific gravity?

   a. 3.0
   b. 0.7
   c. 1.5
   d. 1.3
   e. 1.0

5. In the Sloan-Weir prediction of body density and body fat the measurements required include:

a. skinfold subcutaneous fat measurements
b. anthropometric (bone width) measures
c. muscle circumference measures
d. only 2 of the above (a, b and c)
e. all of the above

6. What is the body density of a subject who has the following measurements:

Ht. = 180 cm.
Wt. in air = 80 kg.
Wt. in water = 2 kg.
density of water at temperature measured = 0.9950 gm/cc
vital capacity (BTPS) = 5000 cc
residual volume = 0.24 x 5000 cc = 1200 cc

a. 1.036 gm/cc
b. 1.028 gm/cc
c. 0.999 gm/cc
d. 1.040 gm/cc
e. 1.021 gm/cc

Answers to Self-Test on Module 19 - Somatotype and Body Fat

1. d correct answer is 19.20%
2. e correct answer is 13.6
3. B = 1,3
4. c
5. a
6. e

SECTION 6

NUTRITION AND BODY COMPOSITION

Self-Test

1. Concerning nutrition:

   1. the diet of an athlete and non-athlete are similar with the major exception of a greater number of kilocalories required by the athlete.

   2. vitamins in the body often play a role as enzymes or catalysts

   3. a normal diet should consist of approximately 15% protein, 55% carbohydrate and 30% fat

   4. particularly for active athletes, it may be advisable to eat more than three times per day

   A = 1,2,3; B = 1,3; C = 2,4; D = 4; E = 1,2,3 & 4.

2. Glycogen loading:

   1. may cause stiffness

   2. may increase muscle glycogen stores from a total body store of 400 grams to 700 grams

   3. may be accomplished by an exhaustive exercise session with subsequent carbohydrate diet

   4. improves anaerobic performance.

   A = 1,2,3; B = 1,3; C = 2,4; D = 4; E = 1,2,3 & 4.

3. Obesity is related to:

   1. number of adipocytes

   2. lipid content of adipocytes

   3. a long term positive energy balance

   4. a lack of physical activity

   A = 1,2,3; B = 1,3; C = 2,4; D = 4; E = 1,2,3 & 4.

4. Endomorphy is characterized by:

   1. linearity

   2. predominance of abdomen over thorax

   3. large bones and thick muscles

   4. roundness and softness of the body

   A = 1,2,3; B = 1,3; C = 2,4; D = 4; E = 1,2,3 & 4.

5. The Heath-Carter somatotype rating is an objective criteria which requires measurement of:

   a. a number of skinfold sites of subcutaneous fat
   b. height and weight as well as ponderal index
   c. bone widths of the elbow and knee and circumferences of calf and biceps
   d. only 2 of the above
   e. all 3 of the above (a,b & c)

6. An object weighed 70 kg in air and 5 kg in water. Calculate its specific gravity (to 2 decimals)

   a. 1.20
   b. 0.93
   c. 1.08
   d. 1.50
   e. 1.00

7. The mean somatotype of varsity football players would probably be:

   a. 1½ - 4 - 5
   b. 6 - 2 - 2
   c. 4 - 4 - 4
   d. 1 - 7 - 1
   e. 4 - 6 - 1½

Answers to Self-Test on SECTION 6 - NUTRITION AND BODY COMPOSITION

1. E = 1,2,3 & 4
2. A = 1,2,3
3. E = 1,2,3 & 4
4. C = 2,4
5. e
6. c
7. e

SECTION 7

SPECIAL CONSIDERATIONS

Module 20

ERGOGENIC AIDS (WORK AIDS)

Module 21

EXERCISE AND TRAINING IN FEMALES

Module 22

TESTS AND MEASUREMENTS

Module 20

ERGOGENIC AIDS (WORK AIDS)

Objectives

Upon completion of this module the student will be able to:

1. Define ergogenic aid. Give examples of possible ergogenic aids.
2. List problems which may be encountered in studying the effects of work aids on performance. Describe a double-blind study. Define placebo.
3. Describe the properties of an anabolic steroid which suggest they may be useful in 'improving' musculature. Outline the conclusion from investigations of the effect of steroids on performance. Identify possible side effects of steroids.
4. Describe the properties of amphetamines which suggest they may be useful in improving performance. Outline the conclusions from investigations of the effect of amphetamines on performance. Identify possible side effects of amphetamines.
5. Define 'blood doping'. Describe the physiological reasoning as to why blood doping may improve endurance performance. Outline the conclusions from investigations of the effects of blood doping on endurance performance.
6. Describe the properties of aspartic acid salts which suggest they may be an ergogenic aid.
7. Summarize the possible ergogenic effects of oxygen breathing prior to, during, or in recovery from, exercise.
8. List sources of Vitamin E. Outline the conclusions from studies on the possible ergogenic effect of Vitamin E.

Reading Assignment

Chapter 20, pp. 437-445.

Self-Test

1. Anabolic steroids

   1. are drugs which are manufactured to mimick the anabolic effects of testosterone

   2. may in some individuals aid in strength gain and increase in lean body mass

   3. may have deleterious side effects, particularly on liver function

   4. are primarily androgenic substances

   A = 1,2,3; B = 1,3; C = 2,4; D = 4; E = 1,2,3 & 4.

2. A number of possible ergogenic aids are listed along with the physiological reasoning behind their possible ergogenic effect. Which statements appear true?

   1. blood doping - may increase number of red blood cells and hence oxygen carrying capacity of the blood

   2. O_2 breathing - taken during exercise may increase the amount of oxygen carried in haemoglobin and dissolved in blood

   3. amphetamines - may stimulate the central nervous system increasing alertness

   4. aspartic acid salts - may aid in removal of ammonia in the blood.

   A = 1,2,3; B = 1,3; C = 2,4; D = 4; E = 1,2,3 & 4.

3. Studies of the effects of ergogenic aids

   1. are complicated by differences in individual responses

   2. are complicated by the fact that the placebo may be a more powerful drug than the ergogenic aid being tested

   3. should be conducted in a double-blind fashion so the experimenter and subjects cannot bias results

   4. are unethical morally and legally.

   A = 1,2,3; B = 1,3; C = 2,4; D = 4; E = 1,2,3 & 4.

Answers to Self-Test on Module 20 - Ergogenic Aids

1. A = 1,2,3
2. E = 1,2,3 & 4
3. C = 1,3.

Module 21

EXERCISE AND TRAINING IN FEMALES

Objectives

Upon completion of this module the student will be able to:

1. Define the performance ratio in comparing athletic performance of men and women.
2. Compare body size and body composition of males and females. Suggest what differences in male-female performances may be related to body size (height, weight) and composition (body fat).
3. Compare females to males in terms of
   a. energy capacity of the ATP-PC system
   b. energy capacity of the lactic acid system
   c. energy capacity of the oxygen system
   For each energy system compare the female and male capacities as absolute values and with correction for body size.
4. Relate the energy capacity differences of males and females to performance ratios of athletic events of different time durations.
5. Suggest why females have a lower max $\dot{V}O_2$ than males.
6. Describe male-female differences in
   a. absolute strength
   b. strength per unit body size
   c. strength relative to muscle size
   Relate these differences to performance ratios in different athletic events.
7. Outline the findings of weight training studies in women in terms of (a) strength development (b) body composition changes and (c) muscular hypertrophy.
8. Compare the suggested endurance training protocol for women to that of men.
9. List physiological changes with training of females, with particular emphasis on any differences in response comparing men and women.
10. Outline the effects of exercise training or sports participation on (a) age of menarche and (b) possible menstrual disorders.
11. Outline the present knowledge regarding (a) performance variations in relation to the stage of the menstrual cycle (b) training and competition during menses.
12. Outline the possible effects of training and athletic participation on (a) breast and reproductive organ injury (b) pregnancy and child birth.

Reading Assignment

Chapter 21, pp. 446-487

Exercises

1. Calculate performance ratios to compare the following male and female results. Interpret the meaning of the ratio.

Event	Men	Women	Performance Ratio
100 m.	10.0 sec	11.0 sec.	
1500 m	4 min 30 sec	6 min 0 sec	
Sargent jump	30 cm	22 cm	

2. Compare the sargent jump results above if corrected for (a) height - where males averaged 180 cm and females 160 cm (b) weight - where males averaged 70 kg and females 55 kg.

3. For a female of 55 kg and a 20% body fat express her max $\dot{V}O_2$ of 2.5 l/min as a function of her body weight and as a function of her lean body mass.

Self-Test

1. With correction for differences in body size, or muscle mass, females compared to males have

   1. much smaller phosphogen stores

   2. a lower capacity of the lactic acid system

   3. lessened strength

   4. a slightly lower max $\dot{V}O_2$

   A = 1,2,3; B = 1,3; C = 2,4; D = 4; E = 1,2,3 & 4.

2. The lower max $\dot{V}O_2$ of women seems related to their

1. lower hemoglobin levels
2. smaller blood volume
3. smaller heart volume
4. smaller muscle mass

A = 1,2,3; B = 1,3; C = 2,4; D = 4; E = 1,2,3 & 4.

3. Women who weight train

1. should expect only small gains in muscular strength compared to men
2. should be prepared to accept the consequence of the masculinizing effect of muscular bulk due to muscle hypertrophy
3. should use relatively less strenuous programs than males since muscle overloading is not necessary for females
4. show increased muscular strength, significant losses of body fat, and a slight gain in lean body mass

A = 1,2,3; B = 1,3; C = 2,4; D = 4; E = 1,2,3 & 4.

4. Women who endurance train

1. increase their max $\dot{V}O_2$ about as much as a male on the same program
2. are highly prone to menstrual disorders
3. may, in some cases, need to take supplementory iron
4. should definitely skip training during menses.

A = 1,2,3; B = 1,3; C = 2,4; D = 4; E = 1,2,3 & 4.

Answers to Self-Test on Module 21 - Exercise and Training in Females

1. C = 2,4
2. E = 1,2,3 & 4
3. D = 4
4. B = 1,3.

Module 22

TESTS AND MEASUREMENTS

Objectives

Upon completion of this module the student will be able to:

1. Describe the difference between real weight loss and water loss due to exercise and health danger signals as a result of water loss.
2. Calculate weight lost as a result of exercise given the caloric expenditure and caloric intake.
3. Describe how real weight may be lost through exercise.
4. Define and describe how the following are measured: dry bulb temperature; wet bulb temperature; black bulb temperature; relative humidity; vapour pressure.
5. Describe a sling psychometer and how it can be used to calculate the relative humidity.
6. Calculate the WBGT index.
7. Show how the wet bulb, globe temperature index (WBGT) can be used to regulate or monitor warm weather exercise and make decisions regarding a team's health.
8. Describe the Margaria-Kalamen Power Test.
9. Calculate an individual's power output (Margaria's Technique), given his weight, the vertical height between the first and last test stairs climbed and the time to cover the stairs.
10. Describe the methods of assessing aerobic capacity both directly and indirectly, on various types of equipment.

Reading Assignment

Chapter 22, pp. 488-512

Exercises

1. Calculate the power output of a subject who ran up a flight of stairs (3rd to last) 110 meters high. The subject weighed 60 kg and he took 50 seconds to cover the distance.

   Answer - see example on page 501 of Mathews and Fox

2. Using the nomogram by Astrand, predict the $\dot{V}O_2$ max of a young boy (age 10) whose heart rate was 150 at a work load of 600 kpm/min. See page 508 of Mathews and Fox.

Self-Test

Select the <u>best</u> answer

1. A black bulb thermometer measures

   a. the temperature of the surrounding air
   b. the radiant energy or solar radiation
   c. the temperature of the air which is moderated by the water vapour pressure
   d. the relative humidity
   e. none of the above

2. Calculate the wet bulb, globe temperature index for the following conditions

wet bulb temperature	80^oF
black globe temperature	140^oF
dry bulb	100^oF

   a. 90
   b. 94
   c. 80
   d. 100
   e. 110

3. What is the power output (in kg.-metres per sec) of a subject who ran up a flight of stairs (3rd step to last) 1.40 metres high. The subject weighed 50 kg and she took 30 seconds to cover the distance.

   a. 10.7
   b. 0.008
   c. 161.0
   d. 433.2
   e. 233.3

4. A good example of an indirect method for estimating aerobic power is the

a. Mitchell, Sproule, Chapman method
b. Saltin-Astrand method
c. Ohio State method
d. Astrand-Astrand Nomogram method
e. Fox Equation method

Answers to Self-Test on Module 22 - Tests and Measurements

1. b
2. b
3. e
4. d

Self-Test

1. A study by Shephard showed that vitamin E administered to athletes over a period of time was responsible for

   1. an improved maximal oxygen uptake

   2. a smaller lactacid oxygen debt

   3. a more rapid heart rate recovery

   4. no significant differences compared to a matched group not given the drug.

   A = 1,2,3; B = 1,3; C = 2,4; D = 4; E = 1,2,3 & 4.

2. Amphetamines

   1. may result in increased alertness and hence improved performance

   2. may result in heart beat irregularities

   3. may result in hyperexcitability, abdominal cramps and blood in urine

   4. are disallowed by the Olympic Committee

   A = 1,2,3; B = 1,3; C = 2,4; D = 4; E = 1,2,3 & 4.

3. Which of the following statements regarding ergogenic aids seem valid?

   1. anabolic steroids may aid in strength gains and increasing lean body mass

   2. anabolic steroids are probably harmless, with no serious side effects

   3. O_2 breathing in recovery seems to be of little benefit either for recovery itself or subsequent work performance

   4. the ergogenic merits of aspartic acid salts have been consistently documented

   A = 1,2,3; B = 1,3; C = 2,4; D = 4; E = 1,2,3 & 4.

4. Which of the following statements comparing male and female performances seem valid?

   1. women are relatively closer to males in swimming compared to endeavours such as running since women contain a greater proportion of fat

   2. women are relatively poor sprinters because of their wider pelvis and small phosphogen reserves per kilogram of muscle

   3. women are relatively poor compared to men in events of two minutes duration since women have a low lactic acid capacity

   4. women are limited in their jumping height because of particularly low muscle strength of the lower body even when corrected for body size.

   A = 1,2,3; B = 1,3; C = 2,4; D = 4; E = 1,2,3 & 4.

5. Comparing average values for non-athletic males and females

   1. women have about 27% fat compared to 12% fat in men

   2. without correction for size difference, the $\dot{V}O_2$ max of women is about 75% that of men

   3. without correction for size difference, general muscle strength of females is about 65% that of males

   4. total haemoglobin and total blood volume of the female is 75% of the values for men

   A = 1,2,3; B = 1,3; C = 2,4; D = 4; E = 1,2,3 & 4.

6. Research evidence collected on female athletes suggests

   1. exercise training seems to result in an upset in the rhythm of the menstrual cycle and a more painful menstruation

   2. that exercise training during pregnancy, because of the hypertrophy of pelvic musculature, inevitably leads to difficulties in labour and delivery

   3. female athletes take an inordinate risk of injury to breast and reproductive organs

   4. the performance of an athlete may be adversely affected during the premenstruum and early menstrual period

   A = 1,2,3; B = 1,3; C = 2,4; D = 4; E = 1,2,3 & 4.

7. A young woman exercised for one hour with an average oxygen uptake of 2 litres per minute and an average respiratory exchange ratio of 0.90 (assume 1 litre of O_2 = 4.90 kcal). If this activity was additional to the woman's daily life activities which maintained a caloric balance (no weight loss or gain), how many kilograms of weight would she lose if she added this activity each day for 2 weeks?

a. 1.07 kg
b. 0.94 kg
c. 25.67 kg
d. 0.04 kg
e. 10.70 kg.

8. A sling psychometer is used to measure the factors used to calculate

a. the vapour pressure of the atmosphere
b. the radiant energy present in the atmosphere
c. the relative humidity of the atmosphere
d. the pH of the blood
e. the barometric pressure of the atmosphere

9. The heart rate of a subject during the fifth minute of cycling at 900 kg·metres per minute was observed to be 140 beats per minute. Using the Fox equation, what was the predicted $\dot{V}O_2$ max in litres per minute?

a. 3.21
b. 3.60
c. 2.89
d. 1.43
e. 8.79

Answers to Self-Test on SECTION 7 - SPECIAL CONSIDERATIONS

1. D = 4
2. E = 1,2,3 & 4
3. B = 1,3
4. B = 1,3
5. E = 1,2,3 & 4
6. D = 4
7. b
8. c
9. b